W9-APD-776

Trust or Consequences

Trust or Consequences

Build Trust Today or Lose
Your Market Tomorrow

Al Golin

Aᴍᴀᴄᴏᴍ

American Management Association

New York • Atlanta • Brussels • Chicago • Mexico City • San Francisco
Shanghai • Tokyo • Toronto • Washington, D.C.

Special discounts on bulk quantities of AMACOM books are available to corporations, professional associations, and other organizations. For details, contact Special Sales Department, AMACOM, a division of American Management Association, 1601 Broadway, New York, NY 10019.
Tel.: 212-903-8316. Fax: 212-903-8083.
Web site: www.amacombooks.org

This publication is designed to provide accurate and authoritative information in regard to the subject matter covered. It is sold with the understanding that the publisher is not engaged in rendering legal, accounting, or other professional service. If legal advice or other expert assistance is required, the services of a competent professional person should be sought.

Various names used by companies to distinguish their software and other products can be claimed as trademarks. AMACOM uses such names throughout this book for editorial purposes only, with no intention of trademark violation. All such software or product names are in initial capital letters or ALL CAPITAL letters. Individual companies should be contacted for complete information regarding trademarks and registration.

Library of Congress Cataloging-in-Publication Data

Golin, Al, 1929–
  Trust or consequences : build trust today or lose your market tomorrow / Al Golin.
    p. cm.
  Includes index.
    ISBN 0-8144-7208-7 (hardcover)
    1. Business ethics. 2. Trust. 3. Reliability. I. Title.

HF5387.G65   2003
174'.4—dc21   *2003009524*

© 2004 Al Golin
All rights reserved.
Printed in the United States of America.

This publication may not be reproduced, stored in a retrieval system, or transmitted in whole or in part, in any form or by any means, electronic, mechanical, photocopying, recording, or otherwise, without the prior written permission of AMACOM, a division of American Management Association, 1601 Broadway, New York, NY 10019.

Printing number

10   9   8   7   6   5   4   3   2   1

Contents

Acknowledgments

First and foremost, I want to thank my "coconspirator," Bruce Wexler, who gave me the push I needed to get this project under way. Bruce has been tireless in helping me organize and synthesize all of the information, research, and interviews, and in bringing my thoughts to life.

Bruce also introduced me to Caroline Carney, my agent, who has been so enthusiastic since she first heard about this concept and who brought it to the attention of Ellen Kadin of AMACOM Books. Many thanks to Caroline and Ellen for their show of confidence in *Trust or Consequences.*

Forty-some years ago when I first met Ray Kroc, the founder of McDonald's, he eagerly embraced the "trust bank" philosophy I outlined to him. The idea of every McDonald's getting involved locally in its community has been part and parcel of McDonald's culture since the early days of its history. From Milwaukee to Moscow, their franchisees have been involved in local charities and causes that have benefited children in need for more than forty years. Thanks, Ray, for thinking big—even when McDonald's couldn't afford to.

The word "trust" has also been part of the credo of my company, Golin/Harris International, and we adopted "Building Trust Worldwide" as our theme. I'd like to thank all the people at Golin/

Harris, past and present, who have made my business life so rewarding for so many years. Rich Jernstedt, the Golin/Harris CEO, has exemplified our culture, and I appreciate his professionalism and dedication for over twenty-five years.

I'd also like to acknowledge the input and research I received from two longtime colleagues—Steve Crews and Linda Leinweber—as well as Bea Witkowski, my assistant of the past fifteen years.

And finally, I'd be remiss if I didn't recognize my terrific wife, June, who likes to say that her main mission these last forty years has been "to keep me humble." She has definitely done a lot more than that—and has certainly earned *my* trust.

Introduction

We had principles when we were poor . . . we certainly have them today, when we're successful.

—RAY KROC

I t has been said that everyone has a book in him. People have urged me to write one for years, arguing that I've been a leader in the public relations field for a long time and had accumulated many wonderful stories and a bit of wisdom. Still, I avoided doing a book, in part because my shortcomings include a lack of discipline and the regimentation needed to get all those sentences to line up and march in an orderly manner across two hundred or so pages.

It turns out, though, that what I really needed was a push to get started. This push involved the corporate scandals that made headlines in the first three years of the twenty-first century.

Enron, WorldCom, Arthur Andersen, Tyco, ImClone, Adelphia, Global Crossing, and others became household names, but obviously not in a positive sense. Even the Catholic Church came under fire not only because of the immoral acts of some priests but because of accusations that higher-up church officials failed

1

to take appropriate action. For a while, it seemed that not a day passed without a headline about some type of corporate shenanigans. Though the misdeeds ran the gamut—financial finagling, CEOs living royal lifestyles while they downsized thousands, product safety problems—one theme kept recurring. In just about every story, the word *trust* appeared. The articles all noted how specific companies were losing the trust of their stakeholders, and how the cumulative effect of all these scandals was to diminish everyone's trust in corporations.

I know something about trust. For over forty years, Golin/Harris International has built a niche in the public relations industry as trust strategists. Clients such as McDonald's, Bayer, Daimler-Chrysler, The Walt Disney Co., Kellogg, Levi Strauss, Lowe's, Toyota, Wrigley, Visa USA, and other top corporations have helped create stronger bonds of trust with employees, customers, the media, the financial community, and other groups. I coined the term "trust bank" to describe how deposits of goodwill can serve a company well when it faces a crisis or other negative news.

Originally, I used this term when talking about the community-related work we were doing for long-term client McDonald's. Over the years, though, we've helped many companies create trust banks, and the goodwill activities have expanded to included everything from internal employee programs to projects involving not-for-profits.

As a result of these experiences, I've learned how companies can build trust effectively. I've also learned how organizations can restore trust when a crisis hits and they need to reestablish relationships with alienated constituencies.

A book seemed the perfect vehicle to communicate the lessons learned. Before I explain how the book will help you create organizational trust, I'd like to describe the other event that pushed me to start writing.

The Trust Survey: Alarming News About Attitudes Toward Organizations

In 2002, Golin/Harris commissioned NFO WorldGroup, a research firm, to conduct a corporate trust survey. It was an in-depth analysis, providing insight into attitudes about trust, factors that influence levels of trust, and opinions about what companies should do to earn trust. In addition, the survey created a "trust index" for twenty-six industries—an index that rated how each industry was perceived from a trust standpoint—based on the following four questions:

1. Whom do you trust the most?

2. Whom do you trust the least?

3. Is your trust in each increasing?

4. Is your trust in each decreasing?

The results of the survey, which was conducted again in 2003, are included in the book as Appendix A, and the trust index as Appendix B.

The results of the survey were tremendously useful and tremendously alarming. On the useful side, they provided insight about what companies need to do to strengthen and restore trust. On the alarming side, they demonstrated that corporations have a long way to go before they're able to strengthen and restore this trust. Our CEO, Rich Jernstedt, put the alarming aspect of the survey into perspective when he said, "Corporate misdeeds—or even perceptions of wrongdoing—cause direct and collateral damage to business as a whole, not only to specific industries. The erosion of trust indicated in the research is a call to action. . . ."

For me, the call to action was to begin work on this book.

Perhaps you'll understand why when I share two of the results with you:

1. Nearly 70 percent of survey respondents agreed with the statement that "I don't know whom to trust anymore" and noted that in the future they will "hold business to a higher standard in their behavior and communications."

2. Of the twenty-six industries surveyed, only five scored in the "Plus" range on the trust index; of the twenty-one that scored in the minus range, the ones with the worst scores were oil and gas (-63), insurance (-59), and brokerage/Wall Street (-58). Other industries with "dangerous" trust index scores included utilities, airlines/travel, accounting, and chemical.

Clearly, companies required help in their trust-building efforts. Either they didn't know how to build trust or were just not aware that they needed to build it.

The survey provided some guidance on what companies should be doing. As you'll learn, one of the themes of this book is that CEOs need to become more involved as trust builders; they need to devote much more of their time to developing and communicating the values and beliefs of the company to all stakeholders. In this regard, the survey asked respondents to imagine they were having a conversation with the CEO of a company they trusted. What would they suggest the CEO do to maintain their trust? Here are the top five responses:

1. Assume personal responsibility and accountability (65%).

2. Personally and visibly show care and concern for customers (60%).

3. Stick to a code of business ethics no matter what (58%).

4. Communicate openly and frequently with stakeholders (56%).

5. Handle crises better, more openly, and more directly (51%).

Similarly, the survey asked respondents what actions companies they didn't trust should take to rebuild trust. Here are some of the answers:

- Be open and honest in business practices (94%).

- Communicate more clearly, effectively, and straightforwardly (93%).

- Visibly demonstrate concern and consideration for employees (83%).

- Make the CEO a spokesperson beyond reproach (50%).

- Be involved with the community (50%).

The survey shows the problems companies are facing and offers some possible solutions. Though I realize that skepticism and cynicism are rampant and that building trust is no easy task, I take heart in how many successful trust strategies we've helped implement. Whether your goal is to strengthen trust incrementally and continuously or you're attempting to rebuild bonds with disillusioned audiences, you can achieve it with the right strategy.

Some companies have done a remarkable job of employing the right strategy. Throughout the book, I'll tell you about these organizations. Here, I'd like to briefly describe the company that has set the gold standard for trust building.

A Credo That Is More Than Words

Since 1999, Johnson & Johnson has received the top spot in the Harris Interactive Inc. ranking of companies with the best and worst reputations. For more than 50 years, the company has been guided by its credo—a statement of values that governs behavior toward employees, customers, the community, and stockholders. This credo is not lip service to vague beliefs; it is a living, breathing document that governs the behaviors of all employees in all offices. Johnson & Johnson is known as being a great place to work, a terrific company to work with, and a good corporate citizen. Its handling of the Tylenol tampering crisis a number of years back—a crisis that I'll discuss in more detail later in the book—exemplified how a company should handle a situation that had the potential to create distrust on a massive scale.

Just as significantly, Johnson & Johnson is an extraordinarily successful company, delivering great results year after year. Whether its success has made its trust-building efforts possible or whether its trust building has led to its success is a chicken-or-the-egg question. Though it's impossible to know which came first, it is possible to state with assurance that its success and trust building have had a synergistic effect.

In 2002, I talked with Ralph Larsen, who had recently retired as CEO of Johnson & Johnson, in an effort to understand how the company had achieved and maintained such an impeccable reputation over such a long period of time. Larsen, who was with Johnson & Johnson for forty years, offered some valuable insights that are echoed by other leaders of companies that have earned their stakeholders' trust.

As I noted earlier, companies that do a great job of creating trust usually are run by CEOs who take their trust-building tasks seriously. Larsen said that when he was first appointed CEO, he met with his key people and told them that when they represent Johnson & Johnson, they're representing more than a trademark.

"You have a 'trustmark,'" he said. "If anybody screws it up, you'll have me to answer to!"

Larsen talked about his trustmark concept convincingly and eloquently to his people as well as to the financial community. He wanted to be sure that everyone understood that they were responsible for maintaining a name that signified more than just quality products.

"We're known as a caring, healing, and curing company, which has been our legacy from the beginning," he said.

The Johnson & Johnson credo and the trustmark concept are universally understood and accepted by the company's employees. Because actions are dictated by these beliefs, the company has been able to respond to problems quickly and without the sort of "cover-your-rear-end" maneuvers that turn off stakeholders.

When Larsen and I were discussing the Tylenol crisis, he said, "Jim Burke, my predecessor as CEO, never hesitated when the decision was made to hit the problem head-on, and fast. We never worried about the cost involved. It was never discussed. It was all about doing the right thing and what was in the public interest."

Finally, Larsen said something that I'm sure would surprise some other CEOs who much prefer strategizing and decision making to "lesser" functions.

"A CEO must put a big priority on communication, internally and externally. I spent a good 75 percent of my time as CEO of J&J telling my vision for the company and motivating my J&J family."

Ralph Larsen and Johnson & Johnson strike me as a good way to start off the book. At a time when many corporations are struggling to rebuild relationships and reputations, Johnson & Johnson demonstrates that it's possible to maintain a high ethical standard and strong values in any environment. Larsen, who recently cochaired a committee on corporate trust, noted that their finding indicated that CEOs ranked just ahead of used car salesmen from the public's perspective. Though I'm going to tell you about companies that have blundered badly and contributed to this negative perspective, I will try wherever possible to include examples like Johnson & Johnson to show what's possible if trust building is approached properly.

Assessment, Action, and Perspective: How to Use This Book

Though I wrote this book to entertain and instruct, I sincerely hope that you will be able to use it in many ways. If you're a CEO or other senior executive, you may find that the material presented here will help you shape a wide-ranging trust strategy. If you're a human resources or communications director, you may be able to use it in a more tactical manner. If you're a younger manager, you may be able to apply the book's lessons to your specific group or team. Some of you may take the lessons learned to create better media relationships. Others may apply the knowledge to specific situations, such as limiting the relationship damage caused by a crisis.

The book is divided into three sections. In the first section—the first three chapters—I'll explore the issues impacting organizational trust today and give you the opportunity to **assess** how your company is doing in light of these issues. Assessment tools include a "degree-of-difficulty" exercise that allows you to determine how difficult it will be for your company to rebuild trust, given the negative events that may have hurt your company. You'll also have the chance to assess what you will gain from your trust-creating efforts—people are often surprised that increased trust translates into benefits that impact a company's sales and profitability.

The second section—chapters 4–8—are the **action** chapters. They correspond to the five steps every company can take to create trust. The "Fix It Before It Breaks" chapter, for instance, recommends a proactive approach and explains how to turn the trust bank concept into action. The "Human Touch" chapter explains how to humanize an organization in ways that create stronger bonds within teams, between employees and management, and with external stakeholders.

The third section—the book's last five chapters—lets you put things in **perspective**. Too often, companies make poor trust-related decisions because they lack a framework for thinking about these decisions. Leaders, especially, are under so much pressure for short-term results that they often err when making choices involving long-term trust issues. The complexity and volatility of the current environment also makes trust decisions problematic. For this reason, I've included chapters that help people think through common trust-related problems. In fact, the first chapter in that section is titled "Tough Trust Decisions," and it will present you with scenarios in which you have to decide what to do when facing situations with no easy answers. You'll also find a matched set of chapters profiling acts of trust and distrust. I've found that it's easier to think about what your company should do when you can evaluate it within the context of what others have done.

All the chapters contain stories. Some involve clients we've worked with. Others involve companies we have no relationship with. Though I've tried wherever possible to name the companies that are the subject of stories, I've included some composites because it gave me greater freedom to illustrate certain points.

The Power of Trust on the Bottom Line

In the pre-Enron era, I doubt that as many people would have been interested in this book. Then, many companies gave lip service to trust building but didn't see it as an integral part of their strategies. In the post-Enron era, most companies see the connection between distrust and results, and how the by-products of distrust—suspicion, anger, cynicism, and disappointment—drive down stock prices, harm employee recruitment and retention efforts, and cause customer defections to competitors.

I hope that this book will help you see the positive connection between trust and results. It's not necessarily a short-term connection but one that reveals itself over time. Companies that work hard at building strong relationships with employees, customers, suppliers, alliance partners, Wall Street, the media, and their communities are the ones that last; they're the ones that enjoy steady growth, solid earnings, and market leadership positions. They're also the ones that, like Johnson & Johnson with its Tylenol tampering crisis, are best able to weather storms. They're able to do so because they repeat my mantra: "Fix it before it breaks." Whenever I hear some executive say, "If it ain't broke, don't fix it," my blood starts to boil. Relationships that are tattered and torn—if not broken—split apart during crises. Companies that make an effort to strengthen their relationships and reputation early on are in a much better position to handle just about any type of crisis. Companies tempted to take shortcuts should remember Confucius's dictum that good government needs weapons, food, and trust. If one cannot hold on to all three, he should give up weapons first and food next. Trust should be guarded to the end, because "without trust, we cannot stand."

Every stakeholder has an expectation of an organization. Employees expect to be treated fairly. Financial analysts expect companies to meet their forecasts. Customers expect packages to be delivered on time. The community expects an organization to contribute to the community in a significant way.

Trust is the belief that a company will do its utmost to meet these expectations, and this book will demonstrate how it's possible for just about any organization to maintain and restore this belief.

People often ask me how I define trust, and I often talk in terms of meeting expectations. Before going on to the first chapter, I'd like you to consider two other definitions that underlie my approach to trust building:

1. Trust is the most basic element of social contact—the great intangible at the heart of truly long-term success.

2. Trust is both a process and an outcome; it's at the heart of dealing with every relationship.

Trust Trends: A Transparent Age, Online Relationships, and a Breakdown in Corporate Values

We are inclined to believe those we do not know because they have never deceived us.

—SAMUEL JOHNSON

"Back in the good old days, people and companies had integrity and real ethics. Not like today."

I hear variations on this refrain constantly, especially after Enron, WorldCom, Tyco, or some other company makes headlines because of alleged misconduct. People talk about how organizations used to stand for something, how CEOs were pillars of the community, how employees were loyal to companies because they embodied values such as fairness and honesty, how organizations treated customers and other stakeholders with consideration and respect.

Nonsense! Business is no less ethical today than it was twenty, fifty, or one hundred years ago. If you doubt this statement, recall the robber barons at the turn of the century, the monopolists like John D. Rockefeller, the virulent anti-Semitism of Henry Ford, the junk bond fiascos of the 1970s, and the Savings and Loan crises of the 1980s. Consider, too, the cavalier manner in which corporate giants polluted the air and water, the many companies that discriminated against women and minorities through their hiring and promotion practices, the lawsuits charging tobacco and automobile companies with covering up health and safety problems involving their products. The list of unethical practices goes on and on.

This crisis of trust we're currently facing, therefore, isn't because business leaders have *suddenly* become amoral or immoral. Instead, it's the result of various trends and events. We're going to look at the major ones so that we can understand why trust has become such a significant issue for all types of organizations. First, though, I'd like to give you an overview of how organizational distrust manifests itself.

More Than Just an Isolated Problem

The results of the Golin/Harris Trust Survey described in the introduction surprised me. Even though I had been working for years helping companies develop trust strategies, I didn't realize how deep-rooted and widespread distrust of business had become. Nor did I realize that this distrust had infected all types of corporate relationships, from the media to customers to vendors to external partners.

Typically, when we think of corporate distrust we think of financial scandals: A company manipulates its financial data for its own ends and investors suffer. It turns out, however, that distrust can arise from many different sources and affect many different stakeholders. Here's a list of possibilities:

- Employees distrust management because it promised not to cut staff for the next two years and then three months later implemented a massive downsizing.

- Customers distrust a company when the company's representatives mislead and manipulate them.

- The public distrusts an industry when companies in that industry are found to have been guilty of unethical or scandalous behavior.

- A community distrusts a company that has been found guilty of polluting the environment.

- Vendors distrust a company when they make certain concessions to be the company's partner but the company doesn't treat them like a partner.

- The media distrusts a CEO who lies to them in order to further his own agenda.

Although organizations do things that create distrust among their various constituencies, distrust can emerge from many sources. Because of the economy or other financial problems, they may have no choice but to downsize. Because of a product defect that they were unaware of, they may receive customer complaints. Because of the unethical actions of one person in their organization, everyone in the company may be viewed with suspicion.

For this reason, building trust is *everyone's* business. It's not just for companies that have committed some public breach of ethics and want to repair the damage. It's not just for companies in a particular industry that the public views with suspicion. In an unpredictable, volatile world, every organization is vulnerable. Without a formal, continuous effort to build internal and external trust, this vulnerability is increased tenfold.

More than one organization that took pride in its great relationships with its employees and its squeaky-clean public image has been blindsided by a trust-deflating event. Crises are becoming routine occurrences for many companies, and the cause of these crises may be a vendor that fails to deliver on its promises, or sudden, unpredictable economic or technological changes that render a company's strategy obsolete. As a result of these events, people start asking questions of companies like:

- How come you didn't anticipate the new technological innovation from your competitor; your last annual report focused on how you were the most technologically advanced company in the industry and pledged to keep the lead no matter what the cost; why did you lie to us?

- Why are you reducing health care benefits at a time when company profits are at an all-time high; how can you justify reducing these and other benefits when I just read that our top executives are among the highest paid in our industry?

Any company can be on the receiving end of these accusations, so companies need to take steps to build trust before a crisis hits. Although trust can be rebuilt at any time, it's much easier to rebuild it when a company has been pursuing a trust strategy from the beginning. This is where a "trust bank" can prove invaluable. Though I'll explain this concept in greater detail later, I want to introduce it here because the philosophy behind it underpins much of my work. As the name implies, a trust bank involves making deposits in an account over time that can be drawn upon when needed. By saying and doing the right things for months or years, a company builds up a certain amount of goodwill that can stand it in good stead when problems develop.

For instance, during the Rodney King riots in Los Angeles, just about every quick-service chain restaurant in Watts was trashed or burned, just about every one except McDonald's. Not a single one of its restaurants was touched. That's because McDonald's had done many things to build strong relationships with the people and institutions in its restaurants' communities. Although hiring the people in these communities to work there was part of this effort, it also created programs designed to help these communities economically, educationally, and in other ways. This goodwill protected McDonald's during this crisis.

More than ever before, companies need this protection. In a transparent age, organizations cannot expect any blemish to go unnoticed.

The Spotlight Is Always On

Trust is a cutting-edge issue because organizations are under intense, constant scrutiny. Not so many years ago, CEOs of even the largest companies were generally unknown to anyone outside of a given industry. Business leaders didn't have best-selling books, corporate scandals were rare, and the public was largely uninterested in the gossip about organizations and their leaders. Nonetheless, there was plenty to gossip about back then, and CEOs and other leaders sometimes got away with murder.

Today our transparent society ensures that companies don't get away with murder. In fact, it sometimes means that companies are convicted of wrongdoing before they receive a fair trial. Let's look at some of the ways this transparency creates corporate distrust.

The Media Microscope

Not only are there more national and local publications covering the business world than ever before, but broadcast media has devoted significantly more airtime to the subject. Cable, especially, has a number of in-depth business programs, and even National Public Radio has developed sophisticated business programming. More significantly, this coverage is far more aggressive than in the past. Witness the many stories pointing the finger at rising CEO compensation in the face of declining company revenues. Or the articles that have focused on rubber stamp boards of directors. Or the ones that have covered CEOs as if they were celebrities, revealing affairs, extravagant lifestyles, and financial wheeling and dealing.

As a result, every misstep of every CEO is magnified. If you were to read only the business headlines, you might think that most companies are run by unethical, greedy, power-mad CEOs. Although some leaders may fit this description, the media's focus on scandal gives the impression that this is the norm. At the very least, it creates a wariness about corporations that touches every-one from employees to customers to the general public.

Certainly the media should expose corporate wrongdoing. But the competitive nature of the news business often causes them to seek sensation over substance. The overwhelming coverage of CEO misdeeds predisposes people to distrust organizations.

Internet News and Gossip

Before scandals and other negative business stories hit the main-stream media, they appear on various Web sites. From Matt Drudge to the May Report (a free-swinging site that reports on technology companies in the Chicago area), the Web often has the worst news first. Rumors of layoffs, mergers, and even wage freezes can be found on these sites. Some top executives have learned about their terminations from online sources before they heard it directly from their bosses. Investors scan numerous sites for every rumor—positive and negative—that might impact their investing strategy.

The Internet often tells us things that mainstream media can't or won't communicate. Many sites don't operate under the same journalistic code as national magazines or television stations, and they are more willing to spread unsubstantiated rumors or take personal potshots at leaders. Sometimes, we fall for the negative gossip about organizations and CEOs, increasing our distrust.

The Internet also makes it incredibly easy to find out anything about anyone. Certainly this can be a good thing, but too much knowledge can prejudice us against an individual or an organization. Every CEO—and every organization—is flawed. When we learn that a CEO was thrown out of Harvard years ago for cheating on a test or that a company discriminated against women in the 1970s, our trust diminishes. Perhaps it should. Perhaps, though, our trust would diminish in *anyone* once we knew every peccadillo he or she had committed.

A Need to Know

As a society, we're as eager as voyeurs to look through the metaphorical window. Transparency is as much a result of our hunger for the naked truth as it is the media's willingness to show it to us. We have an insatiable thirst for gossip about the rich and the famous. We seem to take particular delight in the downfall of powerful companies like Enron and personalities like Martha Stewart. Jack Welch, perhaps the most deified CEO of all time, was the subject of negative story after negative story because of his alleged affair with a journalist. We expect to hear all the dirty details, to be informed about how the mighty have fallen. Perhaps this is only human and a reflex that has always existed, but it seems that we're more hungry for this news today than we were in the past. We used to be willing to allow people some privacy. We used to be proud of highly successful companies like Microsoft rather than eagerly scanning the paper for the latest evidence of their alleged monopolistic moves.

All this is to say that we, with the help of the insatiable media, are more distrustful of organizations in part because we have demanded to know everything about them and their leaders.

The Lack of Real Relationships

I know of an organization that had everything going for it: great products, great service, great people. This technology company, let's call it ABC Tech, was a first-mover in its industry and quickly established itself as the market leader for a few years. Then, as often happens, larger companies knocked off its product and began competing with lower-priced products. ABC tried to match their prices, but still its share of the market eroded.

ABC's three top executives lived in different parts of the country. They had touted their ability to run the company by using sophisticated technology to communicate. They encouraged flex time and telecommuting policies, and it was not usual for managers not to see members of their teams for days on end. Nonetheless, the company had functioned well when it was a market leader, and a number of business magazine stories had praised the company for its progressive, worker-friendly, time-saving policies.

ABC's market eroded in part because of shaky customer relationships. During the company's early years, though, these relationships didn't seem shaky. ABC's salespeople boasted about information systems they made available to customers and how customers could simply plug into ABC's systems to get the data they needed. The problem, of course, was that these systems reduced the amount of personal contact between ABC salespeople and their customers. As a result, when competitors came into the market with lower-priced products, many of these customers felt little loyalty to ABC. The personal relationships that might have convinced customers to give ABC a chance just weren't there. Although ABC's salespeople made a lot of promises about improved services and more innovative products in the pipeline, a number of key customers left.

For this same reason, many employees started looking for other jobs when ABC started losing customers. Though management used the company's Intranet site to convey its confidence in a turnaround, it wasn't a particularly compelling argument or delivered with much commitment. Again, the lack of strong relationships prevented employees from giving management the benefit of the doubt. Although some good people stayed, they struggled because of the "cold" emotional environment. As executives met (they actually gathered in the same conference room!) and tried to create a turnaround strategy, they were stymied by animosity and accusations. One executive accused another of wanting to pursue a particular course because it had been successful for a company he admired. Another executive refused to believe one of the company's founders was sincere in his desire to turn the company around because he had made a lot of money and was more interested in spending time in his beautiful new country home.

ABC eventually declared bankruptcy. With a trust strategy in place, it would probably have avoided this fate. Customers and employees would have hung in longer to see if the ship could be righted. Management would have worked more harmoniously to come up with a viable turnaround approach.

This story points out the problem with a high-tech, low-touch culture. Although most organizations don't have this problem to the extent of ABC, they are becoming increasingly reliant on impersonal communication. People are much more willing to use e-mail than to set up face-to-face meetings or even to talk on the phone. This is part and parcel of the trend toward emotionless interactions that are starting to define business relationships. It's rare to witness the pitched, emotional battles that used to take place routinely not so many years ago. Back then, people used to argue, fight, and make up (at least, they'd usually make up), and the relationships grew stronger over time. Although people didn't always like their bosses or fellow employees, they generally trusted them because of the emotional openness that defined re-lationships.

I fear that because of technology, we soon may be able to avoid real, live conversations. There's a fellow in an office less than thirty feet from mine who regularly leaves me voice mail messages, and I respond by pressing "8" on my phone rather than walking into his office and giving him my opinion. This is like the old radio show in which one of the characters was an anxiety-ridden, door-to-door salesman who desperately hoped that "no one would be at home."

I suspect that many businesspeople love their high-tech tools not just for improved efficiency but because they too hope that no one is at home. They don't want to face sticky situations that might lead to a discussion or even a confrontation.

Perhaps because of political correctness, fear of lawsuits, or a desire to achieve consensus, people are much less willing to say what they feel. Instead of confronting someone about a missed deadline or other mistake, a manager is more likely to leave an after-hours voice mail message or ignore the matter entirely. Al-though this might avoid emotionally messy scenes, it also keeps people at an emotional distance, preventing trust from being built.

Unless a company makes a commitment to humanizing rela-tionships, the online culture will take over. Sophisticated technol-ogy is enticing, and it's easy to forget what's being sacrificed when a culture is overly dependent on this form of communication. Not so long ago, a client called me a dinosaur because I said I didn't believe that everyone was willing to buy products and services online. I maintained that many people preferred to have the ex-perience of seeing and talking to real, live people and seeing and touching the merchandise before making a purchase. Perhaps this is a dinosaur-like view, but with the benefit of hindsight, it's this client and his fellow dot-com companies that are in danger of becoming extinct.

Don't get me wrong. Organizations should value and use all the communication technology at their disposal. What they shouldn't do, however, is let it get in the way of building strong relationships among employees and with customers. Cultures that embrace a certain amount of confrontation and conflict, that regularly hold "town meetings" and reward and promote those people who speak openly and honestly, are the ones that will build trust.

Results Versus Values

The values of companies today are the same as they were years ago. The difference is the current obsession with short-term results. This pressure warps the values of companies and causes them to say one thing to employees and do another. Typically, management talks to its people about the company's values—loyalty, honesty, accountability, and so on—but then acts in a way that runs counter to these values. Managers may give lip service to "the importance of our people" but lop off thousands of jobs when revenues dip slightly. Or they may talk with pride about the quality of the company's products yet buy an inferior grade of material in order to save money and increase profits.

This hypocrisy destroys trust, not only internally but externally. Companies that squeeze vendors too hard or that exaggerate their successes to the media in order to create a falsely rosy picture will alienate people with whom they do business. To a certain extent, this focus on results is understandable. Organizations are under tremendous pressure not only to perform, but to deliver improved performance from one quarter to the next. CEOs may sincerely believe in the values they espouse, but they find it difficult to maintain these values under intense pressure. Some

CEOs may want to build ethical, humanistic cultures, but they're under such intense pressure to deliver short-term results that they downsize unnecessarily and break their promises to vendors. The gap between what these CEOs say and what they do gives rise to distrust.

If CEOs want to maintain the trust of their people and their stakeholders, they need to strike a balance between values and results. In this day and age, this is a major challenge. Years ago, Ray Kroc did a great job of achieving this balance at McDonald's. He could relate to people of all backgrounds and made it a point to talk to everyone. He was a salesman all his life, and he knew how to please people. His charm and genuineness encouraged everyone from employees to customers to trust him. When he said something, people believed he was telling the truth. He was a regular guy. I also believe Ray succeeded because he was a salesman, and he possessed the talent of knowing what his prospects wanted; this translated directly to knowing what his McDonald's customers wanted.

Too many CEOs lack this talent and especially this believability. In part, it's not their fault. They often come from elite backgrounds—prep schools, Ivy League colleges, the top business schools, high-powered consulting firms. There is nothing "regular" about them; they wouldn't know how to sell ice cream to a class of fifth graders. Selection committees favor these candidates precisely because of their background. Although they may be good strategists on paper, they sometimes lack the ability to relate to people from other backgrounds. Their values may be okay, but they don't have the ability to communicate these values to build an environment of trust.

Other CEOs are more down-to-earth and can create trust, but circumstances prevent them from doing so. Any CEO who downsizes, restructures, and outsources is likely to alienate his people, especially if they see these actions as a response to quarterly

profit pressures. Even if a CEO has no other option but these dras-
tic measures, the perception often is that he's taking the easy way
out. At a time when CEOs are being indicted left and right and
unethical executive practices are the subject of business magazine cover stories, it's difficult for people to take CEOs at their
word.

How Has Your Company Responded to This Environment?

Given these trends and events, some companies have taken a pessimistic view, believing there's little if anything they can do to
restore trust in cynical, technologically dependent, short-term,
results-focused times. I've found, however, that there's a great
deal that companies can do. It's simply a matter of knowing how
to create and implement a trust strategy and believing that this is
the right thing to do.

Later, I'll share with you the trust strategy process. Right now,
however, you're probably considering where your company is located on the trust continuum. It's a good idea to do an informal
audit of where your company stands in this area. Answer these
ten questions to get a sense of how well your company has done
at building trust:

1. Does your company have a formal ethics statement? Has it
been distributed to employees? Is it something that people in
your organization back up with their actions or is it merely a "lip
service" document?

2. How do employees perceive the environment in your organization? Is straight talk encouraged or are there repercussions
for those individuals who speak their minds? Is yours a culture
where honesty is rewarded?

3. How do you think your customers, vendors, and other external partners perceive you? In general, do they feel you deal with them fairly and keep your word? Or are your relationships with external groups purely transactional?

4. Has your organization downsized recently? Has it downsized or laid off people more than once in the past few years? Do people view these downsizings as necessary because of financial woes or do they see them as a way to improve the balance sheet in the eyes of analysts and stockholders?

5. Do your CEO and other top executives reflect the values the company espouses? Are they able to balance results and values? Do they withstand pressures to cut corners and people? Do people believe what they say?

6. How honest is the company with employees about its financial situation? Are the company's quarterly and annual reports shared with employees as they are with external audiences? Have you ever presented financial results to employees in town hall–style meetings or in other forums?

7. How has the company responded to a crisis in recent years, especially one that was in the public eye? Was management honest and aboveboard with its statements to the media as well as its various stakeholders? Did management admit errors when it was at fault? Did it look first to confront the issues rather than make excuses or escape culpability?

8. Would you say that relationships between people in your organization have strengthened, weakened, or remained the same over the past five years? Is there an over-reliance on impersonal methods of communication (e-mail, memos, etc.) or is there a lot of face-to-face discussion? Do people feel sufficiently comfortable with each other to speak honestly and directly, even when a touchy subject is involved?

9. Does your culture accommodate the "loyal opposition"? Is there a willingness to let dissident voices be heard? Do people feel free to express opinions that run counter to those embraced by management? Do people feel sufficiently comfortable that they say what they believe rather than what their bosses believe?

10. Is there a concerted effort to create internal and external trust? Is there a formal trust strategy? Has the position of a chief trust officer been created or a trust board (or their equivalents)? Is building trust a priority for management and is management taking action on it?

Though some of these questions may be difficult for you to answer at this point, you should be able to answer enough of them to tell if your company is concerned about building trust, is doing something about it, and is doing it effectively.

When people look at these questions, they often realize that building trust requires work. It's at this point they ask themselves, "Is it really worth it?" As you'll discover, it's worth it from all sorts of perspectives, *including* the bottom line.

CHAPTER 2

More Than a Nice-Sounding Word: The Bottom-Line Benefits

A business that makes nothing but money is a poor kind of business.

—HENRY FORD

Many hard-nosed business folks think trust is a soft value. It's not like a blockbuster new product, a savvy acquisition, or an ingenious cost-cutting measure. Don't make the mistake, however, of equating soft with "unimportant" or "minor." Trust offers organizations benefits that may take time to materialize, but when they do, they can make a huge difference in a company's performance.

Think about my McDonald's story and how its restaurants were spared in the aftermath of the Rodney King riots. What would have been the cost to rebuild twenty restaurants that had been burned to the ground? How much revenue would have been lost during the rebuilding period? How difficult would it have been to lure customers back to stores that the community had destroyed? In this context, trust is a soft benefit that translates into hard dollars.

If you think of the companies that people trust—Coca Cola,

Disney, Johnson & Johnson, General Electric, Apple, Gerber—you get a sense of how much trust can mean to an organization. People are willing to forgive these companies for just about anything within reason: New Coke, the "Lisa" computer, and the Tylenol tampering incident are a few examples. More than that, they're willing to buy products and services from these companies rather than their competitors. Now this last statement comes with a proviso: they're not willing to buy lower-quality products and services or more expensive ones just because of trust. Nonetheless, they may pay a little more for a trusted brand than one without this value attached. They're also likely to remain a long-term customer of a trusted brand than of one that hasn't bothered to build trust.

That's just a quick overview of some external benefits. Internally, trusted organizations have an edge in recruiting the type of people they want to hire. They're also more likely to retain these people for longer periods of time. And they're better able to maintain good morale, even in difficult times.

These internal and external benefits are closely allied. We can see how they fit together when we look at them from a branding perspective.

Two Ways Trust Builds Strong Brands

Branding has become a business buzzword, one that transcends marketing. It's a holistic concept that goes beyond advertising and public relations. Branding has become everyone's business, from the store clerk to the CEO to the human resources executive.

To build a brand, trust has to be an integral component of any strategy. Some companies pussyfoot around the notion of trust, committing instead to "reputation management" or "perception management." Trust, though, involves more than these activities. It drives reputation and shapes perception. It is a bedrock value that impacts the brand in many ways.

Companies intent on building a brand's reputation or perception tend to focus on external stakeholders. Trust, though, begins at home. Employees need to be informed, engaged, and acting as advocates for the company and the brand. If you look at the world's most trusted brands, you'll find that just about all the companies behind these brands have made a strong effort to build trust internally. They've been consistently honest and open in their communications with people at all levels and in all functions; they've created cultures where participation and dialogue is encouraged up and down the line. The strong, trusting relationships that result allow organizations to involve employees in branding efforts. Specifically, they:

- Inform employees about a corporate or product brand repositioning

- Involve people in the promotion and celebration of the brand

- Ensure employees have the competencies, resources, and direction to deliver the brand promise

- Garner employee support of and affinity with the brand identity

- Engage people so they become committed advocates for the brand

With every customer interaction, Internet communication, and product design effort, employees help strengthen brands. This can happen only in an environment of internal trust. Without it, management won't believe that employees are "smart enough" or sufficiently interested to be part of the branding effort. Without internal trust, employees aren't motivated to understand the branding message and show the initiative necessary to communicate it.

Creating a great brand, therefore, is directly linked to creating trust. In fact, our organization has found that trust-based factors are key to effective branding. They include:

- Delivering products and services that consistently meet customer expectations

- Being ethical when dealing with customers and other companies

- Having few if any safety or health-related mishaps

- Making an effort to protect and clean the environment

- Establishing good employee relationships

- Creating a culture of openness and honesty

- Giving a wide range of people responsibility for crafting the image the company presents to the world

- Offering products and services that make important contributions to society

- Providing support for community needs, education, and other charitable causes

Obviously, this list of trust-building factors is wide ranging and ambitious. It involves both internal and external factors, requires coordination of effort, and demands an expenditure of time and money. Building a trusted brand is not for the faint of heart. At the same time, a trusted brand can benefit companies in good times and in bad. In good times, trust can create improved profit margins—people are willing to pay more for brands they trust. In bad times, trust can sustain a company through crises.

Johnson & Johnson's former CEO, Ralph Larsen, recognizes how much a trusted brand is worth; it was why he fiercely protected the company's trustmark during his tenure. Similarly, Larry Light, a world-class management consultant who recently became the chief marketing officer at McDonald's, suggests that no powerful brand can be established without trust.

"A powerful brand is a familiar, quality, leading, and trustworthy promise," he said. "A powerful brand is worth millions of dollars."

Before looking in more detail at the specific benefits trust confers on a company, I'd like to share some stories that demonstrate the form these benefits take.

Beneficial Actions for Companies and Their Communities

Owens Corning, the country's leading manufacturer of home insulating systems, wanted to educate children and homeowners about the importance of making their communities energy efficient. Though it certainly hoped that this effort would favorably dispose homeowners and kids toward its products, the company had a much more altruistic goal. Concerned about the rising costs of home heating bills and about a survey it commissioned that revealed alarming facts about the environment (e.g., that the United States emits more than 20 percent of the greenhouse gases that contribute to global warming even though it has only 5 percent of the world's population), Owens Corning hoped to educate people about a critical issue.

To do so, it hooked up with the Department of Energy (DOE), which launched "Energy Smart Schools" in 1997. This educational program lacked congressional funding and was in need of private sponsors, and Owens Corning became involved a few years later. In partnership with the DOE, Owens Corning launched a number of activities, including:

■ **Energy Smart Schools Invention Contest.** Elementary school students were encouraged to draw an original, energy-saving device and submit a one-hundred-word description of how it worked. Winners received an appointment as an Energy Smart Schools Inventor as well as other rewards.

■ **Energy Smart Schools Inventors Summit.** Winners of the contest met with the nation's top energy scientists to complete and test their energy-saving ideas. This Summit received widespread coverage on the Fox News Channel, NPR, and other media outlets.

■ **A Family Home Energy Quiz.** Teachers handed out a packet of energy-saving activities, including a quiz that students and their parents could take together to determine their homes' energy efficiency.

As a result of these and related efforts, thousands of students across the country as well as their parents became more knowledgeable about energy conservation issues. Through media coverage, millions of people became aware of these issues.

But how did Owens Corning benefit?

First, it linked its name with the DOE, with the Energy Smart Schools program, and with some of the nation's top scientists. By partnering with Owens Corning, these groups communicated their trust in the company.

Second, Owens Corning demonstrated that it was well informed about the energy issues involved. We tend to trust people who know what they're talking about, and some of the educational activities involved information gathered by Owens Corning.

Third, it took a strong stance. People admire and trust companies that have the courage of their convictions. Owens Corning communicated its commitment to helping protect the environment.

It's fair to assume that more people had a better opinion of Owens Corning after this effort than before it. Both kids and their parents could not help registering (consciously or not) that Owens Corning is concerned about environmental issues, informed about them, and doing something to inform others. Obviously, this alone won't build trust in the company, but it contributes to the positive perception of the brand.

Now let's look at how a very different type of company reaped rewards because of its trust-building efforts.

Software company Hot Stuff Corporation (not the real name) was doing exceptionally well a few years ago. It had a number of innovative software products and had marketed them well. Nonetheless, the company's CEO was concerned about a series of "incidents." First, one of the industry's publications had done a profile of Hot Stuff that was complimentary about its cutting-edge products but noted it had a reputation for being arrogant. Second, customer complaints had been slowly increasing over the past year, and they generally related to rude or slow service. Third, some of the company's best software designers had left the company for other jobs.

The CEO, who had founded the company fifteen years ago, felt that Hot Stuff had changed over the years. Though he didn't believe the magazine's assertion of arrogance was accurate, he recognized that the company's success had changed people's attitudes. During the start-up years, the relatively small group of employees had been tight-knit and committed to doing everything possible to meet its customers needs. There was a classic

esprit de corps that seemed missing now that Hot Stuff had fifteen hundred employees.

To remedy the situation, the CEO launched a series of programs and policies, including:

■ **Regular "employee community" meetings** designed to facilitate discussion of issues of concern to employees. These
monthly meetings involved the company's senior staff (as well as
the CEO) and were open-ended forums where no question was
taboo. They often resulted in freewheeling discussions where employees got a chance to air their grievances and fears and management had a chance to respond to them.

■ **A statement of company values** that was more than words
on a piece of paper. The CEO used to believe that such statements
were worthless. He came to realize, however, that many of the
newer employees had no sense of what the company stood for,
and that this affected their behaviors. Values such as compassion,
generosity, and honesty were communicated in a statement and
discussed extensively during the employee community meetings.

■ **Hiring of coaches** for selected individuals who were
deemed valuable employees but whose behaviors were alienating
customers, other employees, or suppliers. The coaching was focused on helping them adjust their behaviors so they reflected
the company's values.

■ **Launching of a corporate identity campaign**, the first in
Hot Stuff's history. The CEO realized that people's perception of
Hot Stuff didn't jibe with reality. Though he accepted that this
perception couldn't be corrected overnight, he decided that making an effort to communicate the company's vision and values
would eventually pay dividends.

Creating trust among its various stakeholders and reaping the benefits of this trust didn't happen overnight, as the CEO had correctly understood. After a few years, though, a subtle but discernible attitudinal shift occurred. An article came out in the same magazine that had implied Hot Stuff was arrogant, only this second article had a much more positive slant, complimenting Hot Stuff's employee community meetings and its values statement. The retention rate of key employees gradually increased, especially among software designers. Service complaints also decreased. Perhaps most significantly, Hot Stuff decided to go public and the IPO went well, in part because it had carved a reputation as a responsible, stable software company. The CEO firmly believed that the efforts had increased trust in the company both internally and externally, and without that trust, the IPO would not have been as successful.

The Benefits List: What Trust Means to Your Organization

From these stories, you get a sense of the range of benefits that accrue to a company that works at building trust. What you probably also grasped was that these benefits come to companies over time. Building trust is *not* a quick fix. Expecting to reestablish great relationships with disgruntled employees by telling them that you're going to implement the bonus policy you've been talking about (but have never implemented) isn't going to do much immediately. One isolated trust-building action won't convince anyone of your sincerity. It takes a number of actions over time to change people's minds and to reestablish trust. That's when the benefits happen.

Don't expect benefits when you've ignored trust strategies for years but suddenly launch one when your company is in trouble. People aren't dumb. They understand that you're trying to deflect attention from some negative event, and they respond cynically to these "cover-ups." When Bill Gates launched his Gates Foundation during the government's antitrust investigation, it was seen by many as an attempt to sway public opinion. Although the foundation gives money to many worthwhile causes, its creation was viewed skeptically in many quarters.

Being proactive, consistent, and sincere in building trust results in the greatest rewards for organizations. Let's look at the types of rewards these efforts yield.

Employee Retention

Certainly trust alone isn't going to keep employees who are woefully underpaid or who are offered great opportunities by other organizations. As we've stated before (and will state again), trust often serves as a tiebreaker. If someone receives a good offer from another company, she may be willing to stay at even a somewhat lower salary because she feels valued and relishes the straight talk and open door policy of the organization. Even in these cynical times, people want to work for ethical companies that value fair play. If management comes across as duplicitous, employees generally feel much less loyalty to the organization than they would otherwise. When you trust your boss (and his bosses) to do the right thing, you achieve a comfort level that's tough to throw away. Most people are reluctant to leave jobs at trust-centered companies such as Johnson & Johnson, Coca Cola, and Disney. In these times, people are worried that their organizations will use any downturn to cut staff and claim they had no other choice. When you work for a company you can trust, you don't have to worry that it will downsize unless it absolutely has to.

People like to work for companies they take pride in. Our firm, for instance, has been very active in a charitable group called the Off the Street Club. We encourage our people to do volunteer work at the club, which benefits kids. We provide them with opportunities to work with the club as well as transportation to get there; we also communicate that we think it's a good thing for our employees to be involved in. It means something to our people that we're strong supporters of this charity. It says something to them about what we value as a corporation, and it's a small but meaningful tool in helping us keep the people who share our values.

Employee Recruitment

It's astonishing how quickly companies develop reputations as good or bad places to work. The Internet certainly has helped accelerate the spread of "buzz" about organizations, and there's so much volatility in the job market today that people invariably know someone who knows someone at the company they're considering working for. IBM is going to have an easier time recruiting people than XYZ Corporation, but when everything else is equal, the company with a values-based culture is usually going to win the recruitment battle over a purely results-based culture. People know which companies treat women, blacks, and other minorities fairly; they are aware which ones have downsized four times in four years; they have heard stories about companies that have gone to extraordinary lengths to help employees who are sick or having other problems. By reading articles, visiting Web sites, talking to friends, interviewing at a company and gauging the atmosphere, people form an opinion about whether a company is trustworthy.

Stock Price/Investing

At the peak of the day trading, dot-com boom, people often invested in companies that seemed to be the next big thing, and little thought was given to these companies' underlying principles. A lot of financial analysts and investors, however, were burned by unscrupulous companies. They witnessed enough

high-flying organizations go down in flames to start asking probing questions about values and beliefs. I remember one young
woman in my office that informed us she was leaving to join a
dot-com company that would double her salary, give her stock
options, and virtually guarantee that she would soon be a million-
aire. Within a year, she was back looking for a job.

I tell this story because everyone knows a story like this one.
Whether they're thinking of joining or investing in a company,
people have learned that there's more to it than immediate financial windfalls. There's a trend toward long-term investing,
and in the long-term, trusted companies do the best.

Customer Relationships

Enron's and Arthur Andersen's much-publicized relationship has
given all organizations and their customers/clients pause. No
longer is the relationship about the best price or the best service.
Although these things are obviously important, other issues have
emerged. Being upfront about problems—and being upfront
sooner rather than later—is absolutely critical. Ad agencies, public relations agencies, and other marketing services providers are
increasingly talking about finding clients with integrity. When interviewing consulting and accounting firms, companies are
screening these firms for past lapses in ethics.

In addition, customer relationships are no longer purely
transactional. It used to be that price was everything, with service
coming in a close second. Today, most people recognize that the
"how" of the relationship is as important as the "what." How
companies share information, how they do what they say they'll
do, how they refuse to cut corners—all of this is integral to trust.
When companies and customers trust each other, they are not
reluctant to share sensitive data or to be honest when something
goes awry.

Partnering

Forging alliances with outside organizations has become critical for many companies. As organizations become leaner, they have a greater need to partner with others. Tasks that formerly were done in-house now require an external partner. In some instances, this involves outsourcing while in other situations alliances must be formed. In both cases, trust makes all the difference in the world. As you probably know, teaming with an outside entity takes guts. It makes companies vulnerable because they must exchange information that was formerly viewed as proprietary. Without trust, these alliances fall apart.

Risk Taking/Innovation

In a culture where intimidation, suspicion, and game playing predominate, employees are reluctant to volunteer their ideas freely. Before offering an opinion or making a suggestion, they reflexively analyze how what they say will impact their job or career. They know that in their culture, a boss may feel threatened by a great new idea or may blame them if their idea doesn't pan out. As a result, they censure themselves, and many of their ideas are never voiced, especially if they entail some risk.

In cultures of trust, people take it on faith that they won't be punished for articulating whatever concept or notion they feel strongly about. Their willingness to venture an opinion that threatens the status quo or that challenges the conventional wisdom is what innovation is all about. In a culture of trust, people believe they will be treated fairly. This means that they will be judged based on their performance rather than their political savvy. This belief frees employees to be creative.

Branding

If you recall the earlier discussion of brands, you'll see how trust can have a positive impact in this area. You may be able to build a solid brand without integrating trust into the message, but it's tough to build a great one without it. Trust gives brands like Gerber, Johnson & Johnson, Volvo, Kodak, and General Electric an edge. In commercialized markets, it says to customers, "Here's a reason beyond price why you should buy our products." Warm and fuzzy sells a lot more products than cold and sharp, and trust gives people a good feeling about what they're buying.

Although there are other benefits to building trust (I'll focus on how it helps companies rebound from crises in Chapter 3), the ones discussed here are significant and have a bottom-line impact. Though that impact isn't always a direct one, it's easy to understand how the indirect effect is substantial and positive.

Does it help you sell more widgets if you have clean washrooms in your company? Maybe not directly, but think about what clean washrooms communicate: that you care enough about your people to make sure washrooms are spotless and that you believe quality is important. Consciously or not, the widget salesperson recognizes that he works for a company that values him as an individual, and the clean restrooms help reinforce this point. He's likely to sell with more effort and enthusiasm for a company that values him than one that doesn't.

How Might Your Company Benefit?

Look at the following list of questions and determine how you might answer them relative to your organization:

- Have you lost talented people in the past year in part because they felt the company didn't live up to promises it made to them?

- Have people told you that they accepted offers from another organization because they felt it was a more humanistic environment than your own?

- Are there people you work with who are fed up with the games bosses play when dealing with employees?

- Does your company make an effort to do pro bono work; does it involve itself in charitable causes and encourage its people to be involved?

- Do you believe your company enjoys a good reputation in terms of its culture and work environment; is it perceived as a place that treats people fairly?

- Do you feel most of your employee programs and policies address the needs of your people (or are they bare bones programs that don't take these needs into consideration)?

- Is it difficult to get top people to join your organization; if so, is it because of low salaries or are there other issues involved?

- How does Wall Street view your company (assuming it's a public company); do you feel it's a good long-term investment?

- Do your customers generally believe that you level with them; do they usually accept your word on most issues (or do they ask for a lot of documentation)?

- Has a customer ever accused your company of being dishonest or unscrupulous in any way; how often have these charges been leveled?

- How many alliances with outside companies has your organization formed in the past year; have these alliances worked out or have they dissolved amid bitterness and accusations?

■ Are people willing to take risks with their ideas and actions; does management encourage fresh thinking; are people generally rewarded for being innovative?

■ Can you honestly say that your brand is considered by most people to be a trusted brand; is it one that conjures up words such as *integrity, honesty,* and *quality*?

You may have difficulty answering some of these questions because they're open to speculation. Still, the point of this exercise is to think about how an effective trust strategy might benefit your company, and after answering these questions, the odds are that you'll be able to come up with numerous ways.

Building Trust Because It's the Right Thing to Do

With all this talk about benefits, I should issue a word of warning: The more you believe in your trust strategy, the more you'll benefit. If you embark on such a strategy with a cynical attitude— you're only doing it because you want to placate people who are angry with you—then it probably won't work. Inevitably, you'll lose interest in building trust because you don't see immediate results. Or you may undertake a trust strategy halfheartedly, and people will quickly realize that your heart isn't in it.

Organizations that create trust among their stakeholders benefit the most because they sincerely believe in what they're doing. They work longer and harder at their trust strategies, and they're more consistent in their efforts. Abraham Lincoln said it best. He was not a particularly religious person, but when someone asked him about his beliefs, he responded, "When I do something that's right, I feel good about it. When I don't, I don't feel good. So maybe that's my religion."

Make building trust your religion, and your company will realize the benefits.

3

The Damage Done: Post-Enron Possibilities

I am different from Washington; I have a higher, grander standard of principle. Washington could not lie. I can lie, but won't.

—MARK TWAIN

At a time when everyone is so disillusioned by and cynical about business, is there anything a company can do to build trust that has a chance of working? Actually, organizations can do a number of things to mend fences and reestablish relationships. The problem, of course, is moving beyond a gloom and doom outlook and recognizing that people are remarkably forgiving.

Doom and gloom, though, does seem to dominate the headlines: another governmental investigation of a leading corporation, another organization laying off thousands of workers, another company accused of polluting the environment. On top of that, your own organization may have lost trust among its stakeholders for any number of reasons.

Rebuilding trust takes savvy and skill, but it's a realistic goal for most companies, especially if they don't panic or make wrongheaded moves.

What Not to Do: Misinterpreting What Trust Building Involves

Some companies like Enron and Arthur Andersen make such horrendous and highly publicized errors that they have little opportunity to regain the trust of their employees and customers. Most companies, though, stymie their trust-building efforts through a series of smaller mistakes. They say and do things that exacerbate rather than offset the cynicism and anger of their various audiences. This certainly isn't their intention, but it's the end result.

In a few cases, management does the wrong thing because of sheer naivete. More often, however, it makes trust-building mistakes because it doesn't really understand how to build trust. As a result, it convinces itself that people will be more likely to trust the company if it denies any culpability in something for which it was responsible. In the short run, management may delay a negative reaction, but in the long run, the truth will inevitably come out and hurt it.

There are also situations where CEOs fail to rebuild trust because they become overly emotional about an issue. A few years ago, an activist group launched a protest against a very large, well-known company that the media picked up on. Though there wasn't a lot of negative publicity, there was enough to anger the CEO. He had every right to be angry, since the group was distributing pamphlets about the company that contained blatantly false charges.

To regain the ground lost because of this demonstration, I advised the CEO to ignore the protest and continue its other trust-building activities. This CEO, though, was a highly emotional guy who considered the company "his baby" and was a passionate defender of it when it came under attack. In certain circumstances, this defense was effective, but not here. If he called attention to the group by responding to its spurious charges, he would just invite increased media coverage and make a bad situation worse. No matter what he said, this CEO represented a very large company and the protesters were a very small group. It would create a classic David versus Goliath scenario.

The CEO wanted to file a lawsuit against the protesters for libel, and my analogy is that if Arnold Schwarzenegger was walking down the street and a child hit him with a pebble, he might be justified in striking back, but it's not what the public would expect of a hero. The analogy wouldn't have made an impact on this CEO, who went ahead with his lawsuit. It cost him millions of dollars in legal fees and probably a lot more than that in negative publicity. Instead of regaining lost trust, he invited public skepticism about a giant company picking on a small, underfunded group. To this day, I'm sure the CEO remains convinced he did the right thing. His attitude reminds me of an ad for car safety I recall seeing years ago. It featured a tombstone on which the following words were carved: "*HE* HAD THE RIGHT OF WAY."

Losing one's objectivity when responding to negative events, therefore, can prevent a company from bouncing back from a loss of trust. Here are some additional actions to avoid:

■ **Focusing only on external fence mending.** Organizations suffer negative publicity and immediately concentrate on assuaging whatever group—financial analysts, government regulators, customers—is unhappy with them. That's fine, but it probably won't work unless a parallel effort is launched internally. Building trust comes from "within." If management has alienated its employees or the culture is one that is highly politicized and secretive, it's reflected in how the company deals with external groups. To change external relationships, companies need to focus on changing internal ones.

■ **Delaying trust building for a "better" time.** More than one top executive has told me that his organization wants to build trust "but we want to wait until the climate for this sort of thing improves." Unfortunately, the climate isn't likely to improve in the near future. Besides, companies that implement effective trust strategies can change the climate, at least the one that surrounds their organization. It's critical, though, for companies to move quickly. The longer organizations allow negative feelings about themselves to persist, the harder it is to rebuild relationships and change their image.

■ **Blaming others for problems.** Neither Firestone nor Ford did themselves any favors by blaming each other for the faulty tires that led to a number of fatal accidents. Saying, "I didn't do it! It's THEIR FAULT!" is a childlike response that won't help reestablish positive feelings toward the company. Trust is built through honesty, frequent communication, community service, dedication to higher ideals, and so on. It is not built by scapegoating or engaging in a war of words with another culpable group. Instead of blaming, companies need to reassure targeted groups that a negative event won't reoccur. When lawyers become involved in these cases, of course, it's sometimes difficult for companies to accept responsibility in public. They often tell companies why they can't do things that would build trust but would also hurt their legal cases. Sometimes there's a middle ground between what's legally proper and what's good for the company's reputation, and I would urge companies to find it when appropriate.

■ **Lacking sensitivity to situations.** Companies are sometimes overeager to build trust, so much so that they act before they think. Creating trust is a long-term process that requires planning and foresight. Imagine if after all the negative publicity about its faulty tires, Firestone had decided to run ads touting a quality award it had just received from an industry group. Though Firestone didn't run such an ad (at least not to my knowledge), other companies have committed equally egregious blunders in a misguided effort to build trust. In the heat of battle, it's all too easy to misjudge people's sensitivities. After Senator Paul Wellstone and his family died in a tragic plane crash, supporters of Walter Mondale's campaign for the vacated senate seat used Wellstone's memorial service to promote his candidacy. Mondale's defeat was certainly due in large part to this miscalculation and the voters' disgust over such poor taste.

■ **Treating the media as the enemy.** CEOs of companies in trouble are often like coaches of losing teams. They blame the media for their failures. As a result, they stonewall reporters or talk to them only when they have good news. We've had clients who, despite our advice to the contrary, insisted on this antimedia stance. As a result, when these companies took positive actions, they didn't receive the type of coverage they deserved. The problem, of course, is that you need the media to build trust. Developing reciprocal, trust-based relationships with editors and reporters is essential if you want them to treat you fairly in print or on the air. Trust has as much to do with perception as reality, and the media shape this perception through *what* they cover and *how* they cover it.

■ **Believing immediate results can cure whatever ails you.** This is often a knee-jerk reaction to problems with various audiences, and it's not limited to financial problems. The idea is that if you reduce prices, customers will forgive you; that if you give people a pay hike, you'll improve morale; that if you give money to a charity, you'll be perceived as a company that cares about people. It just isn't this simple. This quick-fix mentality, unfortunately, is pervasive in our society. In the short-term, it may help companies rebound from trust crises, but the effect is short-lived. You can't keep giving people raises or reducing prices every quarter. You can't keep cutting overhead in order to present a rosy picture to the financial community. Very quickly, these strategies become ineffective.

I recognize how vulnerable every company is to these mistakes and misinterpretations. Years ago, I was working with a CEO who told me that he was going to close a number of his company's unprofitable European banks. I asked him when he wanted to make the announcement, and he said Monday. I suggested to him that this was not the optimum time for such an announcement, since it would garner a great deal of negative press coverage and be the focus of stories throughout the week. Why not delay the announcement until Friday, when there would be less coverage?

The CEO told me he didn't want to appear as if he were hiding bad news; he had made the decision that day, and the earliest possible date to announce it was Monday. He said he realized he might receive some negative media attention, but he also believed that people would appreciate his forthrightness and realize he was taking the best possible action for the company and its shareholders.

He turned out to be right. The financial community applauded his decision for doing what was necessary, *sooner* rather than later. They noted that some CEOs might have delayed the closings and waited until there was some good news to announce along with the bad, but that such an action would have been deceptive and wrong.

I learned a lesson from this CEO. Though it might be counterintuitive to go public with bad news as soon as possible, it's what helps build trust among even the most skeptical people. Although you don't want to be naive and expose all your company's weaknesses and faults at the drop of a hat, you do want to consider full and fast disclosure as a viable option.

The CEO's Responsibility

There's no place for dishonest, secretive, and insular CEOs in this environment. In a more opaque society, corporate leaders could afford to be more manipulative and isolated than they can be today. The 1950s stereotype of the militaristic CEO operating in his ebony tower might have been an exaggeration, but there was some truth to this portrait. Today, such a CEO would have no chance of establishing rapport with diverse external groups or being taken at his word by the media.

To build trust in a transparent society, companies need to be led by men and women whom others consider trustworthy. Just as important, they need to take primary responsibility for building trust. If they foist this responsibility on direct reports, they communicate that they don't believe trust is a particularly important issue. I used to work with John, the CEO of a major corporation, who was a very bright, talented executive, but he considered certain matters "beneath" him. One of these matters involved a controversy over ingredients used in one of the company's products. A competitor charged that the company was using inferior product ingredients in some geographic areas. John thought this was a minor matter and assigned a direct report to deal with it. Years ago, John might have been correct about the relative insignificance of the controversy. In today's climate, however, anything that suggests a company is acting unethically or improperly can quickly turn into a firestorm. That's exactly what happened in this instance, and John's direct report didn't have the experience or authority to handle it effectively.

Part of the problem is that CEOs are selected more for their expertise than for their ability to be open, honest, and communicative. Certainly expertise is important, but sometimes it becomes too important. In this day and age, I'm surprised that boards don't insist that the CEO job specs include traits such as an ability to empathize and a willingness to put other people's

needs before their own. Given the number of CEOs fired for misconduct in recent years, it goes without saying that some people
are selected for the job whom you wouldn't trust to lead you
down the corridor. It's not just that they're unethical or political.
Some people simply aren't communicators or empathizers. They
prefer operating behind the scenes, making deals, and pulling the
strings.

Companies need people like this, but they don't need them to
be CEOs. Can you imagine the corporate equivalent of Richard
Nixon running your organization today? The last thing any company needs is a paranoid, power-hungry CEO, no matter how astute or skilled he might be. This type of CEO makes it very difficult
for companies to create honest and open relationships with their
stakeholders.

We've found that organizations can rebound from all sorts of
negative events and circumstances if they make a sincere effort
to build trust. We've also found that despite the pervasive cynicism about the business world, people are still willing to give certain companies the benefit of the doubt and put their trust in
them. To give you some evidence related to this point, let's look
at three very different examples.

Three Big Headaches

In February 1998, the Chicago utility company Commonwealth
Edison was just about as distrusted as a company could be. It had
received negative publicity for a number of reasons, including the
poor performance of its nuclear power plants and complaints
from consumers about high energy bills. That summer, though,
things went from bad to worse. Numerous power outages, including one that darkened the entire downtown area, earned it the
wrath of Chicago's Mayor Daley as well as consumer protection
groups. ComEd was a dirty word in Chicago, and just saying the
name usually evoked a grimace from listeners.

So it changed its name to Exelon. But that wasn't all it did. The company's chairman, John Rowe, told the mayor, the media, employees, and the public: "I'm absolutely embarrassed over our performance and we're going to fix it and do it as quickly as we possibly can."

Rowe's candor was refreshing, especially after years of defensive responses, pointing fingers at everything from the weather to suppliers and other communication blunders. More significantly, Rowe made a commitment to fixing the problems that had plagued the utility, improving capacity, and modernizing plants. Even more important, he communicated continuously and skillfully about what the company was doing to solve its problems and made himself available to government officials, the media, and his own people. He became a symbol of Exelon's new openness and responsiveness, demonstrating beyond a shadow of a doubt that the company had changed.

Because of these efforts, employee morale rose and public opinion about Exelon turned favorable. *Business Week* cited Exelon as "best utility" and *Forbes* praised the company as "best of breed." In an amazingly short period of time, the utility went from being despised to being praised.

Gallister Inc. (not the real name) is a midsize retailer that was hit hard by the recent economic slump. Before this slump, though, it had a remarkable history of stability and success. A family-owned business originally, the company was sold in the mid-1990s to a public company that the family felt had values and a culture that matched its own. For the first five years, things went well for Gallister. The new owners brought in a CEO who helped the company make a smooth transition, and he continued many of the policies and programs established by the family, such as a better-than-industry-average pay scale, sponsorship of community programs, and employee participation in a number of charitable activities. The culture was very open, and this new CEO kept employees well informed about business issues.

When the economic slump hit, though, Gallister's sales suffered. At first, the new owners dug in and hoped the economy would improve. When it didn't and sales continued to drop, they replaced the CEO with someone who had a reputation for economic turnarounds. This new CEO was given carte blanche to do what was necessary to get Gallister back in the black, and he used it. Not only did he downsize, but he targeted many veteran employees, some of whom had been with Gallister for over thirty years. He also eliminated the charitable and community programs, claiming they were "distracting the company from its mission." And this new CEO was very secretive, keeping most employees in the dark about the company's financial condition and whether further cuts would be needed.

Naturally, morale plummeted. It sank even further when the new CEO began hiring younger people at lower salaries to replace some of the veteran people he had downsized. He also spent a great deal of money redecorating his office and leasing a private jet for his business trips. Finally, management of the company that had acquired Gallister fired the CEO, even though his cuts had improved the company's performance. It realized that the cost of improved performance was too high.

Wisely, management selected a new CEO from inside Gallister, choosing a senior vice president who had been with the company for fifteen years and whom employees respected. It also took the extraordinary step of apologizing to employees for the actions of the former CEO (the chairman of the parent company issued a written memo and also visited the company to apologize personally in a series of group meetings). The new "inside" CEO was able to dissolve much of the anger and resentment that had built up over the last two years. Despite all the negative actions, most employees were willing to forgive Gallister's management for its trespasses. They responded positively to Gallister's trust-building efforts and were willing to give the company a second chance. The company retained most of its best employees and morale improved under the new CEO's administration.

The next story goes back to 1982, but the lesson of this story is as relevant now as it was then. In that year, someone placed cyanide in some bottles of Tylenol Extra Strength capsules and seven people in the Chicago area died. Tylenol and the parent company, Johnson & Johnson, received a great deal of negative publicity initially. In the early days of the crisis, no one was sure who was lacing the capsules with cyanide, and people naturally suspected a Tylenol employee. A trusted name in pain medication quickly became distrusted. In these types of situations, people are so scared and angry that they reflexively look for someone to blame, and Tylenol was a likely candidate. Millions of bottles of Tylenol were pulled from the shelves of stores (and disposed of in homes and hospitals), costing the company a huge sum of money.

Given all this, it's astonishing that only months after this crisis, a poll showed that 79 percent of those surveyed would buy Tylenol again in tamper-resistant packaging. Furthermore, 90 percent of these people said they didn't blame the company for what happened. Within a year of the crisis, Tylenol had once again regained its market leadership position.

Tylenol regained the trust of customers for a number of reasons. First, parent company Johnson & Johnson had lived by its credo for years. This statement of beliefs, which declares that the customer is the company's first responsibility, guided J&J's actions. The company was amazingly open and honest in response to questions from the public and the media. The company's top officers were highly visible and highly responsive. Not only was the product recalled, but new, tamper-resistant packaging was created for the product reintroduction. Advertising was launched with the theme, "Trust us."

The public is willing to forgive even in situations where it might seem that no forgiveness is possible. I would add the proviso that they're more willing to forgive if the companies involved are like J&J and Gallister, organizations that made a concerted effort to build trust before dark clouds appeared on the horizon. This is where the concept of a "trust bank" pays off handsomely.

A Good Investment

In the most basic terms, a trust bank involves "deposits" of good deeds made over time that can be drawn upon when companies face problems. In theory, this means that stakeholders will give an organization the benefit of the doubt in the face of negative publicity or events that would otherwise seriously hurt the company's relationships with various audiences. The organization that consistently works at treating employees fairly, that plays straight with the media, that tells customers the truth no matter what, that is involved in helping the community and in charitable causes is one that knows how deposits in a trust bank are made.

If you've been making these deposits regularly, you'll be able to build trust in any type of industry or rebuild it after major problems. If your organization has never made much of an effort to build trust, I would urge you to introduce this concept to your organization so that you are in a good position to create strong, reciprocal relationships even in the most difficult of environments. You may work in an industry that has been tainted by scandals, lawsuits, and government investigations, but you can still build trust for your company if you make it part of a consistent, long-term strategy.

One company that has made this commitment is Dow Chemical. In the early 1990s, a survey revealed problems with the company's image and employee morale. Though the Vietnam War was long over, the company still suffered negative publicity because of its use of Agent Orange during that war and the stories linking veterans' illnesses with that chemical. In response, Dow made a commitment to building trust internally and externally, and one of the elements of this commitment was a nationwide education program to promote organ and tissue donations. This program was wide-ranging and involved coast-to-coast media tours by leading medical experts, education and video kits for schools, and lobbying efforts to pass legislation aimed at increasing organ donations. The program has earned kudos from congressional leaders and the media, and over time it and other efforts have helped Dow improve its image and its people's morale.

Degree of Difficulty: A Trust-Rebuilding Assessment Tool

Although it's possible for the vast majority of organizations to build trust in the current environment, they don't all face the same degree of difficulty. Organizations like Gerber, Johnson & Johnson, and Apple that have consistently made trust bank deposits are in much better positions than organizations that have just decided that trust is an important strategic issue. Similarly, companies that have received a large amount of negative publicity have a much more difficult trust-rebuilding job than organizations that have been free from scandal or controversy.

Assessing your company's degree of difficulty is a worthwhile exercise. Although it's difficult to make this assessment with precision, you can obtain a general sense of the trust-based challenges that face your company. To help you determine your company's degree of difficulty in trying to rebuild trust, look at the following list of trust-diminishing events and circumstances with a point value attached to each; the higher the point value, the higher the degree of difficulty. See which one (or ones) applies to your organization:

> A major financial scandal involving some form of impropriety—13
>
> A governmental investigation of your organization (e.g., for polluting the environment)—12
>
> A class action lawsuit against your company (e.g., for discrimination against older employees)—11
>
> The resignation or dismissal of the CEO because of unethical conduct—10
>
> A product safety problem—9
>
> A culture where employees feel disempowered—8
>
> A major downsizing—7
>
> Labor problems (anything from a strike to charges of running sweatshops in foreign countries)—6
>
> Loss of significant amount of managerial talent in a relatively short period of time—5
>
> Misleading financial analysts with overly optimistic predictions (that later must be revised downward)—4
>
> Significant customer service problems/complaints—3
>
> Inability to fulfill promises made to employees (such as bonuses, benefit plans, etc.)—2
>
> Product recall—1

Obviously, this degree-of-difficulty table doesn't include all possible negative events. If a negative event impacted your company that's not in this table, you probably can guess the point value that is appropriate given the damage done. Use this table to assign your company a point total. In making this assignment, determine the time period when a given event took place. If it took place within the past year, assign the full point value. If it took place three or four years ago (or more), you can subtract points accordingly. Similarly, you can adjust point totals for the magnitude of damage. If your company was raked over the coals by the media because of a downsizing, you should give yourself the full point value. If there was relatively little negative fallout— the downsizing was handled in a way that was as humanistic as possible under the circumstances—then subtract some points. You'll need to use your judgment. It may be that your company was rocked by a financial scandal but later was exonerated by other circumstances. Or it's possible that your company laid off thousands of workers but hired most of them back within the year. If you feel the circumstances justify subtracting points, feel free to do so. Here is the scale:

> 20 or more points—High degree of difficulty
>
> 13–19 points—Above average degree of difficulty
>
> 5–12 points—Average degree of difficulty
>
> 0–4 points—Low degree of difficulty

Don't be discouraged if you've accumulated a lot of points. Even with a high degree of difficulty, companies can rebuild trust. The key is to approach this challenge strategically and with commitment; the following chapters will give you tools for achieving these goals.

CHAPTER 4

Fix It Before It Breaks

Anyone who has never made a mistake has never tried anything new.

—ALBERT EINSTEIN

"If it ain't broke, don't fix it" is one of my least favorite expressions. It invites complacency. It suggests that if things seem to be working fine, we can sit back and relax.

This is a dangerous attitude, especially when it comes to building and maintaining trust. I know companies that haven't lifted a finger to give back to the community. I know organizations that have ignored building more open relationships with customers. I've seen firms that had not once held a town hall meeting with employees. Their rationale was: Business is good, why should we mess around with this "other stuff"?

In reality, this rationale is a rationalization. They don't want to make the effort to create and implement a trust strategy. Or they don't know how. Or they're ridiculously naive. No matter what their reason might be, they're asking for trouble. Sooner or later, a problem or crisis will surface and it will catch them unprepared. They'll find customers, employees, and other stakeholders doubting their word and looking skeptically at their companies and wonder how all this distrust happened so fast.

The Naive Mindset

Companies should not allow matters to reach such a stage before they embark on trust-building activities. Although companies can build trust after negative events unfold, they will find this challenge less formidable if they've been building trust as part of their business routine. For this reason, fixing it *before* it breaks is the first step of any trust strategy.

Many companies, of course, don't believe their bond with stakeholders is ever going to break. When things are going well, it's difficult to imagine any calamity reversing the organization's fortunes. CEOs look at steady sales, a satisfied workforce, ambitious expansion plans, and the like, and they can't believe they need to do anything to build trust. They think, "People trust us naturally because we deliver the results we promise and we've always been a well-respected company."

This may be true today, but as everyone knows, things change with mind-boggling speed. It's also possible that problems exist that aren't visible to the naked eye, hairline cracks in everything from customer relationships to safety standards. Perhaps a few people in the organization know about these problems, but they're not saying anything for fear of jeopardizing their positions or out of sheer laziness and self-deception.

Large organizations always need people paying attention to trust issues. Even in companies that espouse good corporate values, there's always some issue that is being neglected or handled in a marginal manner. They need to be alert for the warning signs and be willing to take action when they see these signs.

What Does Fixing Before Breaking Really Mean?

You can build trust without a precipitating event like a major scandal or financial crisis. This trust-building step, however, should not be taken lightly or without assessment and planning. You don't just launch the first community-based program that comes to mind or randomly create a flexible employee benefits program to improve morale. These may be good things to do, but they need to evolve from an assessment of the company and its vulnerable points. Companies need to ask themselves: What's most likely to break, even if it seems to be in fine shape now? That's the starting point.

To give you a sense of what all this means, let's look at Dearborne Corporation (not a real name), a midsize pharmaceutical products company. From 1996 to 2001, the company enjoyed relatively steady growth. It had acquired two companies and was eyeing a third. Dearborne's people were paid above the industry average, it enjoyed generally positive reviews from the financial community, and it had received favorable publicity as being a good company to work for. On top of all this, Dearborne had a number of highly promising pharmaceutical products in development.

Management, however, was acutely aware that the situation could change quickly. The CEO had previously been a COO at a large pharmaceutical company that had come under governmental scrutiny for quality control problems. Another member of the management team had been with a company whose service employees, who were part of a union, had gone on strike and created a great deal of negative publicity about the company. As a result, Dearborne's management team was motivated to fix things *before* they broke.

One of Dearborne's more profitable product lines involved hormone replacement medications. Management had determined that this was its most vulnerable area, that a number of studies were ongoing about hormone replacement, and that if any major ones came out showing that this treatment wasn't effective, it could hurt the company's reputation. People could conjecture that Dearborne knew that its product wasn't as effective as advertised—that it had access to research that gave it prior knowledge—and exploited women by selling it and making large profits. Though this wasn't true, in a worst-case scenario, truth wouldn't matter. People would naturally blame Dearborne for marketing a product that had caused more harm than good.

Dearborne recognized that this was its most vulnerable area. Though its assessment revealed a few other issues that might cause it problems—the CEO was concerned about a small but discernible rise in people leaving the company after less than five years of tenure—this seemed like it should be the main priority. As a result, Dearborne began an intensive effort to become more involved in disseminating information about hormone replacement therapy—the company expanded its Web site to include information about alternative therapies and launched a toll-free number for people to call with questions about therapies. Dearborne also allied itself with a major nonprofit group that funded research into a wide range of women's medical issues, providing the group with significant financial support.

These and other efforts cushioned the blow when a major study revealed that hormone replacement therapy was not as effective as previously thought and that it might even do more harm than good. Though sales of its hormone replacement products plummeted, Dearborne's sales of other products directed to women remained strong. Though some pharmaceutical companies received a significant amount of negative publicity after this study came out, Dearborne emerged relatively unscathed. It was not seen as an uncaring, profit-at-any-cost company, and this helped it weather the storm of controversy and maintain strong customer relationships.

Where Are You Vulnerable?

Assessing your vulnerabilities is not always an easy assignment. Sometimes, you don't have any idea that something is going to cause problems until the last moment. Companies are blindsided by everything from employee discrimination lawsuits to environmental problems. In these instances, however, if you've embarked on a generalized trust-building program, you can cushion the blow.

To assess your vulnerabilities, use the "flag" system, assigning a red, yellow, or green flag to the following areas:

- Environmental Issues

- Employee Relations

- Product Quality (including safety issues)

- Customer Service

- Financial

- Local Community Relationships

- Ethics/Morality

- Diversity

- Global (potential problems with offices or plants in foreign countries)

- Legal (potential litigation)

- Restructuring/Downsizing

- Media Relations

There probably will be some overlap in some of these areas, which is fine. The key is to pinpoint the sectors that have a high probability of turning into trust destroyers (red flag), a moderate probability (yellow flag), or a low probability (green flag). To help you make this assessment, ask the following questions:

- Does your organization pollute the environment in any way; has it ever been cited by a governmental agency because of this problem; has the company attempted to stop or reduce its pollution?

- Are your products or services the type where safety is an issue; have you received negative publicity in the past because of a poor safety record and have these issues been resolved?

- Are you aware of any illegal or questionable practices that your company employs to achieve its objectives?

- How likely is it that some or all of your employees might go on strike?

- How many restructurings/downsizings have you had in the past five years; do you anticipate more in the next five years?

- Does your company attempt to balance results and values or does it place short-term performance above all else?

- If you had to articulate a weakness in your corporate culture, what would it be, and how might it lead to problems in the future?

- Is your company generally open and forthcoming with the media or does it favor a policy of secrecy and misdirection?

- Does your organization actively participate in community activities; is it a responsible member of the community?

■ Does management reflect the diversity of your area's population or is its makeup homogeneous?

■ Have you seen any evidence of systemic discrimination against any group in your company (blacks, women, seniors, etc.)?

■ Have you seen a pattern of customer complaints against your organization; is this pattern likely to continue in the future; has your company responded effectively to stop the source of these complaints?

■ Can you see any particular events or situations (a downturn in the economy, a competitor's new product introduction, etc.) on the horizon that might cause your company problems?

What to Do About Your Vulnerabilities

This assessment process isn't an exact science. By posing these questions, you'll simply gain some insight into areas where problems might be brewing. Assign red flags based on common sense. If you're exploiting labor in sweatshops, this is most assuredly a red flag. If your employees are paid less than the industry average, this is a yellow flag.

Based on your red flag issues, here are some ideas for trust-building activities in each area beyond the obvious actions:

Environmental Issues

■ Provide funding for an environmental group that is involved in activities directly related to your company's products and services.

■ Fund research about the impact of relevant pollutants on air and water quality.

■ Sponsor events that foster environmental awareness and education.

Employee Relations
■ Hold town hall meetings that foster a free exchange of ideas and information among employees and management.

■ Provide coaching and other types of training for managers who lack good communication and people skills.

■ Address employee concerns about wages, company policies, and other issues through task forces that, when called for, produce substantive changes.

Product Quality (including safety issues)
■ Offer customers guarantees of quality in one form or another.

■ Join an industry-related quality-monitoring group (or a more general quality management association) and strive to achieve certification at a high level of quality.

Customer Service
■ Retool customer service training to address the complaints and concerns of customers; make a real effort to revamp the training rather than a token effort (a real effort may take more time and cost more money).

■ Provide customers with options for ensuring that their problems are solved and needs are met, from establishing a sophisticated online help service to creating a twenty-four-hour 800 number.

Financial
■ Create an internal system of checks and balances to ensure that no one in the organization can hide financial data or mislead Wall Street and stockholders.

- Make sure the board fulfills its financial oversight role and is alert for any practices that might be considered unethical.

Local Community Relationships

- Establish a partnership with at least one local civic or not-for-profit group in which the company provides financial resources and participates in other ways.

- Become involved in community issues, such as flood control, zoning matters, and education, by encouraging active participation on the part of employees in helping to deal with these issues.

Ethics/Morality

- Create a statement of company ethics or beliefs and communicate the importance of this statement to employees through words and through actions (such as setting up positive and negative consequences based on this statement of beliefs).

- Become involved in causes that dovetail with the company's beliefs; establish a job position or team responsible for finding appropriate charities, not-for-profit associations, and other good causes with which the company can be involved.

Diversity

- Make a formal effort to create diversity at all levels of the organization; identify areas that lack diversity and recruit with this goal in mind.

- Implement diversity training to help people appreciate cross-cultural and other differences.

Global (potential problems with offices or plants in foreign countries)

■ Assess the working conditions of offices and plants outside the United States to determine if they meet acceptable levels in terms of wages, working conditions, age of workers, etc., and make the necessary changes to bring them up to acceptable levels.

Legal (potential litigation)

■ Be proactive in dealing with individuals and groups that have animosity toward the organization; work with them to resolve differences and meet them halfway in an attempt to achieve a reconciliation.

■ When conflicts with individuals and groups threaten to spiral out of control, focus on reaching a settlement rather than winning; do everything possible to defuse a tense situation and avoid the type of name-calling and public battles that diminish trust.

Restructuring/Downsizing

■ Treat downsizing as a last resort; consider and implement every possible alternative before cutting staff.

■ When downsizing can't be avoided, do everything possible to cushion the blow both for those who are let go and for those who remain; communicate honestly and openly with employees about the reasons for the downsizing and the hope that this will not happen again in the near future; provide outplacement, fair compensation, and other resources to people who are downsized out of jobs.

Media Relations

■ Make a consistent effort to establish open, two-way relationships with the media; provide them with ideas and information on a regular basis and be responsive to their requests.

■ Create editorial roundtables and other events that demonstrate your willingness to share information and your expertise in a given area.

These trust-building activities are necessarily generalized. In real life, companies face very specific vulnerabilities based on everything from their industries to their cultures to their competitive situations. A trust strategy must be based on these and other factors. Nonetheless, the trust activities listed here will give you a sense of the wide range of options available to you.

You should also keep in mind that you may have more than one vulnerability, and numerous trust-building opportunities present themselves. Realistically, most companies can't or won't embark on numerous activities simultaneously because of cost and manpower requirements. That's why it is essential to prioritize what needs to be fixed first.

Prioritizing is a matter of determining where the biggest potential "hurt" might be. Obviously, red flags demand a higher priority than yellow flags. If you have two or more red flags, the best way to determine which area needs the most attention is projecting worst-case scenarios. What would happen if a foreign government shut down your overseas plant for safety violations? versus what would happen if an activist group launched a boycott of your company because it felt you discriminate against minorities?

As you hypothesize about these worst-case scenarios, evaluate the following:

■ **Extent of Damage.** In other words, is an incident or situation such that there's extensive damage to the company's reputation, or is it more limited? In many cases, it's not that difficult to project how a given problem might impact a company. You know the damage from a long employee strike will probably be more extensive than a few employees filing a lawsuit against the company for age discrimination. Although both are serious problems that should be addressed, the first priority should be the effects of a long-term strike.

■ **Internal/External Impact.** Prioritize scenarios most likely to have both internal and external effects rather than just internal or just external.

■ **Length of Time Damage Might Last.** Some problems are likely to blow over quickly while others will linger. Consider whether a specific problem or incident will last for days, weeks, or months. As a general rule, the answer to this question can be determined by the next factor on this list.

■ **Media Coverage.** Is the worst-case scenario likely to receive major or minor headlines? Can you see coverage extending beyond a one-date hit and becoming a continuous story? Does the scenario involve the type of scandal or breach of ethics that makes headlines?

To a certain extent, prioritizing trust-building activities is a judgment call. If you talk about the previous questions with other decision makers in your company, you'll probably encounter a variety of viewpoints. Still, it's better to go through this analysis and debate than to make arbitrary decisions about where to invest your trust-building energy.

How to Make Trust Bank Deposits

You've read about how companies like McDonald's and Dow Chemical reaped tremendous benefits by adopting fix-it-before-it-breaks programs. They made extraordinary efforts to "do good" without anyone forcing them to. Instead, they were motivated by a desire to be good corporate citizens, to help others in need. They also had faith that these efforts would strengthen relationships with various communities—relationships that they wanted to strengthen even though they weren't weak. This is what the trust bank is all about. By making deposits of "good works," these companies raised the level of trust among their stakeholders. If a problem occurred—such as the riots in Los Angeles—McDonald's could draw on the relationships the company had built to see it through the time it took to resolve the problem.

The trust bank concept is flexible. It can be used by organizations in many different ways, from meeting the needs of individuals and groups inside the company to helping out individuals and groups in the community.

People always ask me how to create a trust bank, and I explain that the specifics depend on the situations. As you've learned, your trust-building efforts need to flow from the particular problems, opportunities, and events that your company faces. With that written, however, I would add that trust bank programs generally share the following criteria:

■ **Commitment.** If you're going to launch a project to assist a not-for-profit group or to lobby for meaningful legislative initiatives, you can't approach it like it was a mundane matter like changing coffee suppliers. People will sense if your organization is sincere in its desire to help others or if its motives are suspect. Commitment means that your organization understands the issues involved and is emotionally as well as intellectually committed to the project. To achieve this commitment, people need to take the time to educate and involve themselves. They need to read, to participate, and to contribute time and ideas. It's not just about giving money, but about doing something that individuals within the organization believe in.

■ **Achievable Goals.** If your company wants to build trust, it won't tilt at windmills. Companies that declare they're going to start a campaign to "feed the hungry" or "cure cancer" often get caught up in impossible quests where they have no impact. Noble but vague goals aren't going to register with people. You'll find your stakeholders will appreciate your efforts if you create programs that can achieve meaningful results. This means concentrating on feeding the hungry in your community rather than in the world. It means addressing employees' concerns about health care rather than trying to lobby for universal health care. People remember when you achieve your objectives.

■ **Targeting.** Make your trust deposit in the right bank. In other words, do something that is meaningful to your target audience. What particular stakeholder group is of greatest concern to you? This is the group that needs to be "touched" by your trust-building efforts.

■ **Ownership.** United Way is a good cause but offers a company little opportunity for individual recognition. The ideal trust bank program offers a company strong identification possibilities. You want to create your niche, whether it's being the first to sponsor some sort of innovative employee career center or being the only company involved with a particular charitable group.

■ **Self-Interest.** This may seem like a contradiction, but no one expects your company to be completely selfless. People understand that you have certain products and services you sell, and they'll accept that your trust-building efforts will benefit these products and services in some way. The key, though, is to choose an activity or project that makes sense, given what your business is all about. If you're in the plastics manufacturing business, it makes sense for your company to become involved in funding research activities designed to limit the environmental impact of plastic waste products. This is in your self-interest and in the interest of the public. If, on the other hand, your plastics company decides to become involved in funding diabetes research, you'll be viewed as interlopers—you're getting involved in an area with no relevance to your organization.

■ **Synergy.** Rather than going it alone, you should consider partnering opportunities. By joining with another organization, you can combine your resources to have a greater impact. Many times, this involves for-profit companies partnering with not-for-profit associations. McDonald's is partnering with the World Wildlife Fund to develop "Wecology," the largest environmental education effort offered to educators. This program showed teachers and students that McDonald's is a company concerned about finding solutions to environmental problems.

■ **Cost Sensitivity.** You can build trust without breaking the bank. It's a mistake to think that the amount of trust you build is directly proportional to the amount of money you spend. Be responsible in how you spend your money. Donating a billion dollars to a charity may seem like you're trying to buy a good reputation.

■ **Newsworthiness.** If no one is aware of the good things you're doing, you won't create much trust for your organization. But this isn't just about getting your company's name in lights. By sharing the news of what you're doing, you attract attention to good causes and worthwhile activities and you also inspire others along the same lines. Therefore, avoid me-too activities and programs. Be creative in your choice of trust bank projects and look for attention-getting forums in which to implement these programs. Holding a news conference to announce your donation isn't particularly newsworthy. Creating an unusual event or anything out of the ordinary stands a much better chance of attracting the media's attention.

■ **Employee Involvement.** Obviously, if your trust bank program is focused internally, employee involvement is a given. But if you're focusing your efforts externally, you should make sure the program involves employees. Don't just assign implementation of the program to a three-member team. Find ways to give employees incentive to participate and give them opportunities to do so. Surveys show that these involvement efforts boost employee morale, self-esteem, and job pride.

Ms./Mr. Fix-It: The CEO's Role

It's very difficult for companies to fix what isn't broken if their CEOs are arrogant. Leaders who run companies in an imperialistic manner refuse to acknowledge vulnerabilities, let alone do something about them. Part of this is *tradition*. For many years, CEOs were schooled to hide weakness and project strength; they saw their roles in militaristic terms. For this reason, it has been hard for these old school CEOs to take trust building seriously. Even younger CEOs, however, adhere to this mindset. They honestly believe that compassion, empathy, and other humanistic traits are of secondary importance. Someone once told me, "Never mistake kindness for weakness," and I think this is the mistake arrogant CEOs make.

Many CEOs seem to shed their "normal" personality and put on their CEO game face the moment they walk into the office. I've known CEOs who are genuinely warm and humble human beings in their personal lives, but the moment they arrive at work, they think they need to be macho. They can't drop their armor for even a moment, and this prevents them from recognizing the value of building trust.

Many of these coldly objective CEOs come out of the financial or engineering areas. Both functions tend to produce emotionally neutral decision makers who rely exclusively on facts. Engineering and financial CEOs fix things when they break based on indisputable evidence that things are *really* broken.

I'm not suggesting that CEOs be soft and fuzzy types or that they should be indecisive or lack pride in their organizations. It's just that I've known top executives who have dismissed preventative trust maintenance as unworthy of their attention; it's too soft and fuzzy to merit their attention. They honestly believe that if the company loses trust because of an incident, they'll be able to repair the damage quickly. As smart and successful as these leaders might be, they underestimate the difficulty of rebuilding stakeholder trust.

They also underestimate the importance of frankness, honesty, and the ability to see things from other people's perspectives. Lee Iacocca, the former head of Chrysler, was brilliant at anticipating problems and solving them before they spiraled out of control. He didn't just fix a broken company, he kept it from breaking again. Like many great salespeople, Iacocca worked hard at building trusting relationships. Through his television commercials for Chrysler, in meetings with financial analysts, and especially in his interactions with the media, he built relationships that served the company well in the long run. I was on a media tour with Iacocca, and I marveled at his skill in Q&A after a news announcement. He loved the interplay with reporters, and they loved him because of his openness and candor. He fixed the relationship with media before it was broken, and he did such a great job of it that Chrysler enjoyed largely favorable press coverage during Iacocca's tenure and even after he was gone. It wasn't that the media distorted the truth but that they gave Chrysler the benefit of the doubt; they believed that Chrysler spokespeople were leveling with them, and their stories reflected this belief.

CEOs aren't always like Iacocca, in part because they surround themselves with people who refuse to level with them. This may be because they adopt the imperialistic CEO demeanor, and people are too intimidated to tell them bad news. You can fix things before they break only if you have people who are willing to say, "I know our numbers look great now, but I'm anticipating a downturn in the coming year because of what's happening now in the European financial markets." It's tough to give the CEO bad news when things seems to be going well, but *that's* the time when it's best to hear the bad news.

A number of years ago, I went to a dentist who was an old family friend, and he was a wonderful storyteller, so I enjoyed going to him. When I told him my gums were bleeding, he responded that I shouldn't worry about it, this happens to everyone at some point. I was relieved that it wasn't a problem. When they were still bleeding months later, I went to another dentist who told me it was a big problem, and I ended up needing major periodontal work. Too many CEOs prefer surrounding themselves with people like the family dentist. When I hear someone say, "No problem," I often suspect that it's no problem now, but a big problem later.

The Good News: Some Companies Never Leave Well Enough Alone

Though Levi Strauss has experienced some problems because of increased competition in its industry, it has managed to survive and thrive because it has been proactive about building trust. I personally witnessed one small but telling example of this attitude when I visited its headquarters in San Francisco a few years back. In the lobby, Levi Strauss had set up a booth and was distributing information about AIDS. Manning the booth was the CEO of Levi Strauss. This wasn't just a token appearance. He was there for the entire day, completely engaged in the process of informing people about the disease and advances in treatment. A culture of caring for employees and customers has been a Levi Strauss hallmark throughout the years, and its CEOs have done a great job of communicating the culture through their actions.

Another proactive company is Toyota. In June 2001, our public relations firm was brought in to help it manage a difficult situation involving Reverend Jesse Jackson and his Rainbow/PUSH Coalition. Reverend Jackson and Operation PUSH had taken offense at one ad that Toyota was running and had informed Toyota that they were examining all aspects of Toyota's diversity policies. Though Toyota had pulled this ad even before being approached by Reverend Jackson and had an excellent record in terms of diversity, it recognized that this small incident could easily be blown out of proportion and hurt its reputation.

Certainly one option Toyota could have taken was to do nothing and let this small storm blow over. It wasn't guilty of any wrongdoing; it had not discriminated against anyone. Toyota had simply run one ad in questionable taste that the company had quickly decided to pull.

Yet Toyota's management astutely realized that this incident with Operation PUSH could be an opportunity to strengthen its diversity program rather than simply a problem to be ignored or treated superficially. Diversity had always been an important issue to Toyota—after all, it is a Japanese company with American plants and a huge, multinational customer base—and it decided to use Operation PUSH's complaint as a catalyst to strengthen its diversity leadership position.

Toyota launched a multidimensional program to achieve this goal. It developed and communicated a diversity plan that superceded the issues that Reverend Jackson had raised, doing such things as identifying the current diversity program's best practices and rolling them out through all its companies. The plan was announced at the annual Rainbow/PUSH conference and received a great deal of positive publicity. In addition, Toyota set up a Diversity Advisory Board that included well-known political and civic leaders, empowering them to meet quarterly and oversee the implementation of Toyota's plan.

Toyota fixed a small crack in its foundation before it spread. It acted with speed and commitment to deal with a relatively minor problem that could have turned into a major trust-breaking nightmare if handled poorly. By acting proactively, Toyota created more trust rather than maintaining its reputation and relationships.

Trend Spotting: A Good Preventative Talent

If there's any fix-it-before-it-breaks skill that a company might target, it's the ability to predict how an emerging trend or event might impact the ability of others to trust the company. You don't have to be a psychic to exercise foresight. Some people are keenly aware of a multiplicity of trends and can make the imaginative leap necessary to see how these trends might impact the company in adverse ways. Cereal manufacturers like Kellogg, Quaker Oats, and General Mills, for instance, seemed to have been aware that the rising health consciousness in this country might bring them flack because many of their cereals contained little or no fiber and a lot of refined sugar. As a result, they not only introduced more health-conscious cereals, but they made a point of emphasizing the nutritional benefits of their cereals on their packaging and in many other ways. As a result, these cereal manufacturers didn't experience the loss of confidence and trust from their stakeholders they otherwise might have, if they hadn't spotted this trend.

Tobacco companies, on the other hand, ignored the growing animosity toward smoking for years. They never really believed

the early signs that cities would outlaw smoking in public build-
ings or that cancer victims would successfully sue tobacco companies or that they would come under attack for trying to "hook"
teenage smokers. They *refused* to face these issues until they
could no longer ignore them, and by then they had lost a great
deal of trust. When these trends first surfaced, the tobacco companies were extraordinarily profitable and the attacks against
them were sporadic and poorly organized. Though they were
going to lose some degree of trust no matter what they did, they
could have lessened the impact by being more proactive and honest in confronting the health ills caused by smoking.

United Airlines, too, must have learned early in the game that
it wasn't doing as good a job as many other airlines with on-time
arrivals and departures. It was only late in the game, however,
that it began working to correct this problem and making passen-
gers aware of its efforts. Although there were many other reasons
for the airline's bankruptcy filing, this was one thing it could have
controlled and contained. It wasn't simply a matter of becoming
a more efficient airline, but of bending over backwards to inform
customers when flights were late, explaining why they were late,
and providing some sort of compensation when this happened.
Instead, United was hit with massive amounts of trust-breaking
publicity because of its poor on-time record.

A few years ago, I went to a client's national convention attended by thousands of employees. When I walked the floor, I
saw a sea of white faces. I was astonished by how few blacks or
Hispanics worked for the company. I mentioned this observation
to the CEO and suggested that the homogeneous composition of
his company could make him vulnerable. The CEO responded
defensively that "We hire people based on their ability; race
doesn't enter into it." That may have been true, but the lack of
minority representation was glaring and seemed like it would
eventually cause problems. The CEO rebuffed my suggestions, in-

sisting that there were more "significant" problems that he needed to deal with. A year or two later, though, when his company was attacked for discriminatory hiring policies, he probably felt differently.

Though there's no magic to trend spotting, it does require an ability to scan a large amount of diverse data and grasp how seemingly unrelated events might conspire to impact a company negatively. For instance, a few studies have recently come out noting the increase in obese children. A politician or two has spoken out about this problem. It's possible that in a few years if this trend continues, it may have a major impact on a number of types of companies. The obvious ones are snack food manufacturers, but less obviously, the impact might even be felt by everyone from car manufacturers (who court younger drivers, depriving them of weight-reducing exercise) to computer manufacturers (who hook kids on video games where they don't get any exercise).

Organizations will be in a much better position to fix things before they break if they devote time and people to trend spotting and analysis. Too often, this is an informal activity in companies or one farmed out occasionally to consultants and researchers. Why not create a trend-spotting team composed of a researcher, an analyst, and a strategist? Together, they could anticipate developments that might create friction with stakeholders. Companies talk all the time about the need for "vision," but what they also need is this type of foresight.

CHAPTER 5

If You Can't Do It, Please Say So

The price of greatness is responsibility.
—WINSTON CHURCHILL

Many organizations, when they *can't* do it, don't say so. Instead, they "overpromise," convinced that this is a better alternative than risking the loss of a customer, an employee, a deal, a flattering article, or a favorable analyst rating. Although overpromising may buy some time, it almost always comes back to haunt organizations. Failing to deliver on raised expectations is the kiss of death, at least in the long term. It's much better to disappoint people right away with honesty than later when they discover you misled them.

Perhaps a better way of putting it is: You're better off pleasantly surprising people with good news later on than giving them unrealistic expectations too soon.

Organizations build trust not only by fixing things before they break, but by being consistently honest about what they can and cannot do. This may seem self-evident in theory, but in practice, companies overpromise in many different ways. Let's look at the various types of overpromising, why companies do it, and how to end this practice before it creates distrust.

A Wide Range of Exaggerations, Unfairly Raised Expectations, and Outright Deceptions

Perhaps the most common type of overpromise revolves around making a sale. Promise them anything and worry about how you'll fulfill that promise after you've landed the business. Companies rationalize this type of sales pitch six ways till Sunday, telling themselves that *everyone* exaggerates in order to make a sale and that it is expected selling behavior. In reality, though, most people remember what is promised and hold companies accountable for delivering on what they "guaranteed" during the presentation.

Our agency once pitched an egg producer association at a time when many stories were being written about how the cholesterol found in eggs was bad for the heart. During our presentation, we talked about how we would emphasize the importance of eating eggs in moderation as part of a healthy diet. We did not, however, promise that we would convince the media that there were no health risks to eating eggs or that we could counteract the conclusions of recent studies. Another agency did take this approach—it promised the moon and the stars—and the egg council chose this agency. Six months later, it fired the agency because it was unable to communicate the message that eating large quantities of eggs was a perfectly healthy thing to do.

An instructive postscript to this story occurred after the other agency had been selected. One of the members of the egg council knew people at our agency, and he asked why we were so "pessimistic" during our presentation. We told him we weren't pessimistic, but we were being realistic and didn't want to promise what we couldn't deliver.

One category of overpromising, then, involves selling situations. Here are some others:

■ **Financial Forecasts.** Wall Street is unforgiving when companies promise results that never materialize. More than one CEO has talked rhapsodically about the next quarter in order to cushion the blow of the current dismal quarter. They may do a good job of convincing analysts that a company's fortunes are on the upswing, but if this upswing never occurs, analysts are furious. Wall Street hates surprises, and it hates unnecessary surprises even more.

■ **Employee Retention.** To keep good people, managers will often guarantee them promotions, new job responsibilities, raises, and bonuses. In some circumstances, they do so because they want to retain employees during a particularly busy period. In other instances, they make these promises hoping they can keep them but knowing that it's not likely. In either situation, word spreads quickly in companies when false retention incentives are used. If this type of practice is condoned in an organization—whether explicitly or implicitly—it causes employees to doubt *everything* management says.

■ **Recruiting Guarantees.** This can be a great temptation for companies pursuing "hot" candidates for top positions. Knowing that these superstars can have their pick of jobs and may well have other offers, organizations will offer all sorts of perks and promises. The rationale may be that once they're onboard, they're not going to leave if the company fails to live up to all of its guarantees made during the recruiting process. Perhaps, but it's unlikely that this individual will ever trust management again, and he or she may become the sort of cynical boss that spreads distrust among other employees.

We once were interviewing people for a top position in our

company, and we found someone who seemed like he'd be a great fit. During our conversations, this candidate made it clear he wanted to be moved up to another position six months after he joined us. We could have told him that this was a possibility, but we'd have to evaluate his performance after six months before making this decision. If he turned into a top performer, we might have kept this promise. But it was something we didn't feel comfortable doing because we didn't think it was likely that it would happen. We had other people who had been with us for years in line for the position he coveted, and they would have been rightly disappointed if they weren't at least considered for it before we handed it to this new person. So as much as we thought he would be a valuable addition to the company, we told him we couldn't agree to his terms and ended up losing him rather than overselling him.

■ **Deadlines.** Companies tell regulators they'll meet federal or state requirements by a given date; they tell customers that they'll have the order delivered on the target date; they insist to the financial community that they'll be profitable by a given quarter. For all these groups, the dates are important. They're counting on deadlines being met, and when they aren't, they often feel deceived. This is especially true when it seems as if organizations had no intention of meeting the deadlines and merely agreed to them because of ulterior motives. Too often, we underestimate the importance of due dates, acting as if being late by a day, a week, or even a month won't make that much of a difference. It might not make a difference in the greater scheme of things, but it sends a clear message that a company doesn't honor its promises. If a company isn't serious about its deadlines, what *else* isn't it serious about?

■ **Deal Negotiations.** Some organizations are known as great dealmakers, but they may not be known as particularly honest or fair negotiators. In mergers and acquisitions, in labor negotiations, and in joint ventures, some companies consider themselves clever bargainers because they cut the best deals. They are willing to say anything in order to close the deal on favorable terms. To convince a company that an acquisition would be good for both companies, they paint a rosy picture of the future, all the while knowing that they intend to cut 25 percent of the acquired company's staff. The sour taste these dealings leave in people's mouths is the residue of trust gone bad.

■ **Media Interviews.** It's astonishingly easy for otherwise intelligent leaders to become carried away during media interviews. They start pontificating about their company's great prospects and before they know it, they've painted an unrealistic portrait of those prospects. Stories like this not only unfairly raise an audience's expectations, but they also mislead reporters. When reporters write an article or broadcast a story that later turns out to be inaccurate, they feel burned by the individuals who gave them inaccurate information. Consequently, they don't trust CEOs and their organizations, and their subsequent stories are likely to reflect this lack of trust.

Three Types of Overpromising

Saying you can do it when you can't is motivated by everything from greed to false optimism. Organizations as well as individuals may firmly believe that they can achieve what they've guaranteed, but they're simply deceiving themselves. They may also be Machiavellian in the way in which they use glowing words to manipulate others. Although there are many reasons behind false promises, let's look at the three most common varieties.

First, there's the *arrogant* form. This is embodied in the adage, "No one ever went broke underestimating the intelligence of the American public." This is dead wrong. No only can you go broke, but you can go broke in a painfully public fashion. Just ask the leaders of companies that tried to pull the wool over people's eyes.

Nonetheless, I've known powerful leaders who were convinced that no one would ever call them on their statements. They were so sure that people would either forget what they said or would forgive them for saying it that they felt free to make grandiose pronouncements. They proclaim to their employees that their company is going to set the standard for creating a truly diverse, multicultural company, and then a year later it's still the same predominantly white company (especially at the management level) that it has always been. People are smarter than arrogant leaders think, and they're certainly smart enough to *distrust* a leader who makes a major promise and then ignores it.

Second, there's the *magical* incarnation. People make great promises because they somehow believe that if they say it, it might come true. You've heard CEOs give rousing speeches, saying, "This is going to be the best year we've ever had," even though they're aware of the factors that might make the year less than stellar. With good intention, they're attempting to raise morale. But the bad effect of all this is rising expectations that often aren't met by reality, leaving people bitter and disappointed when the year doesn't go well. CEOs and other leaders can be carried away by their enthusiasm and optimism, but just wishing it doesn't make it so. Although it's great to give people a goal to shoot for, problems result when they're misled about what's possible.

Third, there's the *fear* factor. Leaders are afraid that people will be initially disappointed when they tell them that they're not going to get the position, that they can't begin the project for another year, that the order won't arrive within a week, that the results won't be what they expected. They don't want to deal with the negative emotion when these people hear disappointing news; they don't want to confront the sadness and anger. To avoid it, they fudge the truth. They tell an employee hoping to get a raise that "I can't say it's a sure thing, but it's a good possibility." They tell a customer who is on her third call complaining about a late order that "it definitely will be there by tomorrow" in order to defuse that anger. This technique may take the emotion out of the air at first, but it will return with much more force when a reassuring response turns out to be nothing but an overpromise.

Here's a story that illustrates this last point. A while back, one of our clients, the head of Corona Beer in the United States, was coming to Chicago, and I decided I would take him to lunch. I had my assistant call my club to make a reservation, but I told her to make sure it served Corona Beer. When my assistant called and explained the situation, the person who answered assured her that it did indeed sell Corona.

At the club, a rather haughty waiter came to our table, and when we asked for two Coronas, he replied that the club didn't carry "that brand." With a certain amount of anxiety—the Corona executive didn't seem pleased—I asked the waiter to check and make sure, knowing that he was mistaken. A few minutes later he returned with two bottles of Corona.

After the meal as we were leaving the club, I saw the maître d', and I told him about how the waiter had mistakenly thought they didn't carry Corona. The maître d' explained that he knew what must have happened. He said that there had just been a wedding reception in the club, and the married couple must have ordered Corona specifically. Ordinarily, he added, "we don't carry that beer."

He said this after I had introduced him to our client and noted that he was the *head* of Corona.

With hindsight, I realized that when my assistant stipulated that the club must have Corona if we were going to eat there, the club employee must have feared losing a customer, remembered the wedding, and decided to tell my assistant that the club stocked Corona. This made everyone happy initially, but I was mortified later on. Although it wasn't a malicious deception, the result of even this small overpromise diminished my trust and damaged my relationship with this client, who didn't have much of a sense of humor, and didn't respond well when I tried to make a joke out of the incident.

How to Say You Can't Do It

Certain organizations are known as straight shooters. They've earned reputations among stakeholders for valuing truth over saving face or covering their rear ends. Everyone from customers to employees believes them when they say they can't do something—and when they say they can. These companies recognize that surprising people with good news is infinitely preferable to giving them unrealistic expectations.

Although a trade-off is involved, it's a trade-off worth making if your goal is building or restoring trust. Admittedly, it's not always easy to say it straight, especially when what you say can have major repercussions such as winning or losing a customer or receiving high or low marks from financial analysts. If you believe that raising expectations can help you come out on the winning side, you may wonder: "What harm would it do to stretch the truth? Though we don't think we can give them exactly what they want, who really knows?"

Resist this type of thinking. It's what gets companies into hot water. Although no company is simon-pure and it's unrealistic to expect all employees to tell the whole truth all the time, leaders need to make an effort to be straight with their stakeholders as much as humanly possible. If they want to build trust, this is the only option.

To help organizations resist temptation and speak the unadorned truth, here are five steps to take when you have to deliver
difficult or disappointing news:

**1. Explain the odds of achieving what the other person/
company wants.** Most of the time, the choice is not between "yes
I can" and "no I can't." Generally, what needs to be said occupies
a gray area. Companies get into trouble when they consistently
lean toward the bright end of the spectrum even though the facts
don't justify this optimistic position. In fact, being honest means
saying, "There's about a 30 percent chance we can deliver what
you want" or "In six months, we doubt the situation will change,
but in a year, the odds are good that it might." Most people respect those who frame their statements in terms of probabilities.
This fosters realistic expectations and communicates the reasons
behind these expectations.

**2. Communicate as early as possible when a promise can't
be kept.** There are times when promises are made sincerely but
circumstances change and they're no longer realistic. The temptation may be to delay delivering bad news, hoping against hope
that something will happen to make the promise viable once
again. Don't give into this magical thinking. Whether the promise
has been made to a customer, an employee, the media, or anyone
else, companies have the responsibility to correct misperceptions
as soon as they're convinced they are misperceptions. It's terribly
difficult to guarantee a customer that a new product will be available on a given date and then hear from the factory there's been
a production snafu that will delay things by a month. The sooner
you inform this customer of the snafu, however, the better your
chances of maintaining his or her trust. Too often, customers hear
about these problems later from other sources, and when this
happens, they rightly feel betrayed. Delaying bad news to the last

possible moment might be human nature, but it's not good for maintaining open, honest relationships. The earlier someone knows you can't deliver, the easier it is for him to make alternative plans. This decreases the disappointment caused by your failure to deliver.

3. Put the news in context. Many times, when you can't do something, there's a reason for it. It may not always be a good reason or a reason the other party will understand or appreciate, but it's worth articulating. The recipients of your news may empathize with your plight—a sudden departure of a key employee, weather problems that delayed a shipment, a computer glitch. They may have been in the same or a similar situation themselves, so even though they're disappointed at what you're telling them, their disappointment is moderated by their empathy. At the same time, don't turn the context into long-winded excuses. Although people might empathize with your situation, they don't care about your excuses. Don't rub salt into the wound by going on about the once-in-a-lifetime snowstorm in California that delayed the package. Create the context quickly and succinctly. If you talk too much about why you can't do what you say, people immediately become distrustful. As Shakespeare wrote: "Methinks he doth protest too much."

4. Make it personal. Although the communication here is usually between representatives of the same company or of two different organizations, a personal relationship exists between individuals that shouldn't be ignored. Therefore, don't deliver the news by e-mail, regular mail, fax, or phone if at all possible. Face-to-face communication demonstrates that this is too important to deliver in any other manner. A less direct form of communication conveys that you have something to hide or that you've done something wrong and literally don't want to face up to it. If you're sincere about apologizing for a lapse, let the other person sense your sincerity—a difficult objective if she can't look you in the eye.

In addition, make sure the right person is delivering the news. This is not a responsibility to delegate to a direct report. Nonetheless, I know a number of instances when executives had disappointing news to deliver and they assigned this task to subordinates. Imagine how you would feel if your boss had promised you a raise at the end of the quarter and his assistant told you it would not be forthcoming. In most cases, you'd feel that you weren't valued and would look for another job. Or consider if you were a reporter who had written and published a story based on a CEO's inside tip and had then received a call from a direct report saying that the CEO "feels that she may have misled you about some of the facts." Given the impersonal nature of the CEO's communication, the reporter won't take anything this CEO says at face value.

Biting the bullet and dealing directly and personally with other people is difficult in these situations, but it's the type of behavior that helps maintain trust.

5. Create a dialogue around the news. Don't just announce bad news. Instead, create an exchange of information and ideas around it. Sometimes bad news announcements arrive in the form of letters, memos, e-mail, and press releases. Other times, the announcement is made verbally at news conferences, analyst meetings, or other forums. An announcement without dialogue is like a slap in the face. It communicates that the other party isn't worth the time or trouble of a conversation. Though that message may not be the intent, it's the inference that's often drawn.

Of course, a dialogue around a difficult subject is something many people want to avoid. Who wants to get into a conversation about how your company blew the deadline or can't give the union what it said it would give it? These can be heated dialogues, but they're preferable to the cold and impersonal feeling of announcements. Think about professional athletes who are traded to other teams and bitterly remark that they had to "read about it in the papers." They'll never trust owners and coaches who promised them that they'd let them know if there were any possibility of them being traded and talk to them about it first. A dialogue wouldn't have changed the outcome but it could have kept the relationship intact. Sports teams that make a habit of announcing bad news through the media gain reputations for being insensitive to players' needs and often fail to attract free agents.

Dialogue gives companies the opportunity to capitalize on relationships that have been nurtured for months or years. Sitting down with another person and hashing out the issues can clear the air or at least provide an opening to rebuild the relationship at some future point.

It's Not Just What You Say but How You Say It That Counts

It's much easier to accept disappointing news when it's delivered with humility and empathy than when it's dismissive or arrogant. Too often, managers in organizations become defensive when they have to level with employees or customers about mistakes they've made. Or they work in highly politicized cultures where it's unacceptable to show weakness or admit culpability. Or the managers are egotistical and need to assert their superiority, preventing them from swallowing their pride and admitting that they're not capable of doing what someone else wants. For these reasons, they say things like:

Well, maybe we made a mistake, but it wouldn't have happened if you would have given us the information when we asked for it.

We're the market leader. If there's a problem, its source is somewhere else on the supply chain.

Perhaps to you this is a difficult deal, but I've negotiated far more difficult agreements than this one, so I have no doubt it will go smoothly.

Defensiveness, arrogance, and boastfulness all multiply the negative effect of overpromising. People who are down-to-earth, straightforward, and pleasant not only find it easier to tell people what they can and cannot do, but their personal style makes it much easier for other people to accept what it is they have to say.

I know a CEO who typically opens his talks to financial analysts and other groups by admitting a mistake he made. This isn't an act. He is a genuinely humble person who isn't embarrassed by or ashamed of his errors. He feels it's what makes him human, and he doesn't want anyone to think he's some type of superior human being just because he's a CEO of a major corporation.

His manner gives him instant credibility. People naturally assume that if he's big enough to admit his mistakes right off the bat, he's not going to mislead them later. You want to believe what he says and forgive him for what he's done wrong. Jimmy Stewart frequently played a character with this aw-shucks sensibility, and it was tremendously endearing. With this CEO, it's no act. Financial analysts are used to CEOs making absurdly optimistic projections and boasting about future accomplishments. When this leader starts out talking about how he missed the boat on a new technology or implemented a flawed strategy, it creates great credibility for him with financial analysts.

I'm not suggesting that everyone suddenly start talking and acting like Jimmy Stewart. For some people, this would be an unnatural style. Everyone, however, can be sincere and unpretentious. This basic style will help your audiences accept what you have to say with greater understanding and tolerance, even if what you're saying isn't the best news in the world.

6

The Human Touch

We don't stop playing because we grow old; we grow old because we stop playing!

—GEORGE BERNARD SHAW

It's very difficult to build trust in an antiseptic environment, no matter how "professional" the people are or how successful the company is. Though I've talked about trust from a strategic perspective, creating it is not purely a business process. Without empathy, flexibility, and humor, trust won't grow.

In a company of workaholics, there's not sufficient time or interest to build relationships. In a results-obsessed culture, the focus on short-term profits makes it a minor crime to do anything that doesn't contribute to profitability. In a strict, by-the-numbers organization, the flexibility necessary to meet people's diverse needs doesn't exist.

Show me a company where employees go through the day wearing grim-lipped expressions and I'll show you a company where suspicion and pessimism rule. To create and maintain trust, you need to humanize your organization in ways both big and small. Let's look at why this humanizing process is especially important today.

It's Hard to Warm Up to Cold Efficiency

Years ago, organizations had as many ruthless CEOs, manipulative executives, and cruel bosses as exist today. The difference is that back then, human interaction, individuality, and achieving a balance between work and fun were higher priorities. Companies take themselves too seriously today. It's almost as if they feel they're on some sort of mission and must sacrifice their time and pleasure in order to achieve a sacred goal. As a result, they find it difficult to loosen up, to get to know the people they work with, and to laugh at themselves.

I recall making a presentation at Maytag, a company with a long and glorious history. We entered the huge, walnut-paneled conference room, the walls lined with oil paintings of the company's patriarchs. We were presenting to the company's top executives, and they were seated in the room's plush leather swivel chairs when we arrived. After shaking hands, I went to sit down in one of these chairs, and as I sat down and leaned back, I found myself tumbling backwards. Amazingly, I managed to do a backward somersault and right myself. Even more amazingly, *no one said anything!* These people were wound so tight that no one asked if I was okay or commended my surprisingly acrobatic performance. It was as if acknowledging that something unbusinesslike had taken place was bad form. When I said, "And now for my next trick . . ." no one even smiled, except for the people from my own office.

This overly serious attitude is more prevalent now than ever before. Perhaps it's because the business stakes are higher or the competition is fiercer, but whatever the reason, it does not lend itself to creating trust. It's not unusual to talk to executives or even younger employees who say they work ten hours a day six or seven days a week. Or to find people who routinely don't use all (or any) of their vacation time. Or to have lunch with a manager who talks only about business issues and doesn't reveal a single personal detail about himself—or ask a single personal question of you. In these overly serious settings, people feel subordinated to the work. In these companies, it's difficult to have heart-to-heart conversations with your boss or for people to take customer or vendor relationships beyond a transactional basis.

Another problem is the lack of face-to-face time. I know one large company where the four top executives all live in different parts of the United States. Many of their meetings take place online, and they are rarely all in the office together. I've noted how e-mail and other online communications can be abused, but it's not just technology that's to blame. Companies are outsourcing many assignments that used to be handled in-house. Global travel forces people to communicate by phone and e-mail rather than in person. Because most companies are running leaner, people have more to do and less time for the type of lunches and extended conversations that foster relationships. In short, the atmosphere isn't right in many companies to nurture the exchange of ideas and emotions that form a foundation for trust. When you don't really know someone, it's difficult to trust him.

You've probably also worked for or visited companies where people don't seem to be enjoying themselves. Sometimes these organizations are highly political and people are always watching their backs. In other instances, the companies are run by dictators where employees hate coming to the office each morning. Working in what feels like a totalitarian state makes it difficult to be friendly or concerned about others. Just as significantly, working in an unpleasant environment makes it difficult to generate much empathy or kindness from "outsiders." If employees go around feeling beleaguered and fearful, they're not going to inspire much trust from customers, suppliers, the community, or the media. The way employees behave toward external groups reflects the company's culture. If it is the type of culture where the strong bully the weak, then the weak will often bully suppliers and be fearful of customers.

All this is not to say that companies with oppressive or unpleasant environments can't be successful—for a while. Just as totalitarian regimes sometimes rule powerful countries, organizations where individual rights are trampled still can be profitable. I'm sure, however, that these environments will eventually cause them problems. A few years back, I went to Bentonville, Arkansas, to visit Wal-Mart's corporate offices. I found the headquarters to be especially Spartan. Perhaps that's putting it kindly. In most corporate offices, you find at least a few aesthetic touches or employee-centered features—there is artwork, a sense of playfulness in what is displayed, visual manifestations of what the company is all about, pleasant lounges, or other types of employee recreation areas. You might also hear music or animated conversations among employees.

There was none of this at Wal-Mart. It resembled nothing so much as a movie version of corporate life from the 1950s, one that showed a vast room of cubicles with employees hard at work and unwilling to even look up from their computers. I confided my observation about the environment to one of the Wal-Mart people we were meeting with, and she told me that she agreed it was depressing, and that if it wasn't for the great stock options Wal-Mart offered its people, she'd be gone tomorrow.

I realize it's unfashionable to say anything negative about a company that has been so highly praised—and it's possible that I misinterpreted what I observed or that things have changed since I was there—but I wonder how this atmosphere will impact hiring and retention at the giant retailer if its fortunes take a turn for the worse. Without the great stock options and other financial incentives, how loyal would Wal-Mart's people be?

Respecting employees as *individuals* is what generates trust. When employees feel that the organization truly cares about their growth as employees and their hopes and dreams, they respond in kind. Southwest Airlines is often mentioned in the same breath as Wal-Mart as one of the world's most successful organizations. I was traveling from Dallas to Houston recently on Southwest and I was trying to make a tight connection at the airport when I was delayed by security. I must have looked worried about making my connecting flight because a member of the Southwest staff approached me as I was rezipping my bag and offered her assistance. She escorted me to my gate, expressing concern about my situation, reassuring me that I'd make the flight, and joking about the delays. I felt that this person really cared that I made the flight, and I know she would not have communicated this feeling unless she worked for a company that cared about her. From this and other experiences with Southwest, I can say that I trust it to get me where I'm going safely and on time more than other airlines.

I'm not sure what Southwest does to engender this attitude, but I suspect it bears similarities to the practices of a company that was recently profiled on *60 Minutes*. SAS is a North Carolina–based software company with nine thousand employees and $1 billion in sales that makes an extraordinary effort to treat its people with respect, honesty, and appreciation. Here are just some of the things it does for its people:

- Provides a 50,000-square-foot, state-of-the-art fitness center

- Encourages people to get their work done in a thirty-five-hour week and allows them to work a flexible schedule

- Provides four SAS Montessori day-care programs at one-third of the normal cost

- Offers free medical care from the SAS medical staff

- Has social workers on staff to help employees deal with "life" issues

- Has two staff artists who create artwork for display within the company

SAS has never had a bad year or laid off a single employee. Its people are paid well, and the result is amazing loyalty in an age and in an industry noted for high turnover. In the software industry, an average of more than 20 percent of employees leave their employers annually. At SAS, the turnover rate is 3 percent!

SAS is a private company, and its CEO, Jim Goodnight, acknowledges that he can treat his employees far more humanistically than a CEO at a public company can. In the *60 Minutes* interview, he is quoted as saying, "There is not trust anymore in public companies. I think it's an excellent time to be private."

Though it may be easier for a private company to offer the perks SAS provides, a public company can build trust just as a private one can. I would amend Goodnight's assessment that there is no trust in public companies to there is less trust in the wake of restructurings, downsizings, and financial scandals. The important point, though, is that every CEO is capable of demonstrating the same sort of respect and caring for employees as Goodnight has exhibited. It's just good business!

Humanizing the Organization: How to Create a People-Centered Environment

If your company is like most organizations, it probably treats people decently but not exceptionally. Most companies aren't dictatorships or utopias. Instead, they're somewhere in between. In this gray area, employees have mixed emotions about the company. They may like one policy and resent another. They may believe they're being paid fairly but resent all the rear end–covering paperwork that is part of the culture. Or they may think the company does a good job providing them with retirement plan benefits but is unconcerned about offering a good family healthcare plan. Many times, people feel their organizations are hypocritical: They talk about how employees are one big family, but when they deny them access to information and decision-making input and dictate transfers to offices in other geographical locations, there's nothing family-like about it.

Realistically, companies need to strike a balance when it comes to humanizing their organizations. They have limited resources and can't give employees everything they want; the extensive list of perks SAS offers isn't affordable for many companies. Downsizings and restructurings are a fact of life, and there are going to be times when individual employee needs are going to be sacrificed for group goals. Therefore, the steps I'm going to suggest here aren't designed to shoot your company to the top of the "best companies to work for" list. Instead, the objective is to create both formal and informal policies that increase the bedrock humanity of your company. In addition, I'm assuming that you already know that nothing you do in this regard will matter if your people feel they're not being paid fairly or promoted when they deserve it. If you create a great benefits policy but pay employees like slaves, you're not going to get many humanizing points.

With that in mind, here are some relatively easy things any organization can do to create a kinder, gentler culture:

■ **Encourage rapport building.** If you've ever taken a class in sales, you know that one of the first things they teach you is to identify with your prospects and customers. If a customer is interested in music, you talk to him about a concert you recently attended and ask him what concerts he's been to lately. This is such a simple thing, yet I've seen very smart executives talk to direct reports, customers, suppliers, and the media without any sense of how to build rapport. Some of them talk only about themselves while others only issue orders or ask questions about an assignment. Most of these people aren't boors or egomaniacs, but they have never learned how to establish good relationships in a business context. They may grasp relationship building in their personal lives, but at work they take on a business role and lose that very human part of their personality.

Although you can't legislate rapport building, you can encourage it through basic training sessions. Traditionally, companies have viewed this sort of thing as appropriate only for salespeople. In reality, it's the people in finance or the MIS group who often need it the most. Just making them more conscious of the need to build rapport would make them better executives, let alone better people.

It would also make sense to encourage this behavior by making it an evaluation item on performance reviews. There are bosses who don't know a single thing about their direct reports beyond their particular competencies; they focus entirely on knowing an individual's strengths and weaknesses. It's no wonder these direct reports feel like pawns rather than people. If managers are evaluated based on how well they connect with individuals—both inside and outside the organization—they'll make more of an effort to engage in dialogues rather than monologues.

▨ **Help people feel comfortable.** Are your people uptight, anxious, or stressed out? Because employees are under more pressure than ever before, organizations need to do whatever they can to reduce this pressure to an acceptable level. Besides monitoring workloads and making sure people have adequate time and resources to accomplish their tasks, companies can take other steps to make sure that employees feel comfortable in their working environment.

Sometimes little things make a big difference in how people feel about work. Casual dress, for instance, has been embraced by those tired of the "office uniform." You wouldn't think that freedom from formal outfits would mean so much to employees, but it does. It's almost as if they feel the organization is giving them permission to be themselves, which affects their attitude toward work and their relationships with people inside and outside of the office.

There are many ways to increase the comfort level of employees, such as providing them with a pleasant work space, allowing them to talk on the phone or with coworkers without feeling they're doing something *wrong,* or offering them a lounge with free refreshments, music, and television. I brought up the casual dress topic because it demonstrates how a simple policy that costs nothing can impact employee attitudes. I also brought it up because I had something to do with starting the casual dress trend.

A number of years ago, I went to Hawaii on business and met with an executive from a local communications company. I arrived Thursday night, and Friday morning I went into the lobby of the hotel where I was staying to meet this executive. He arrived wearing an "aloha" shirt while I was wearing my business suit. Though I didn't say anything about it, I noticed that most other businesspeople I met were similarly attired. Thinking, when in Rome, do as the Romans do, I shopped for an aloha shirt over the weekend and arrived at my client's office on Monday wearing it. To my surprise, he and everyone else in his office wore suits. He explained that "Aloha Friday" was an island custom, allowing people to get ready to have a head start on their weekends.

When I returned to Chicago, I met with Ray Kroc, and he told me about his idea of wanting to institute early Friday closing hours during the summer at McDonald's offices. I then related my Hawaii experience and suggested that allowing people to dress casually on Fridays might enhance his idea. He agreed, and photos of McDonald's executives wearing casual attire received a tremendous amount of national publicity and no doubt influenced many other companies to institute casual Fridays.

■ **Give people options.** One work size doesn't fit all. Companies that accommodate the different work styles and preferences of employees (within reason) are responding appropriately to the increasing diversity of the workforce. Here is just a sampling of the ways companies can attempt to provide options:

- ■ On-site day care

- ■ Telecommuting

- ■ Job sharing

- ■ Flexible hours

- ■ Liberal transfer policies

- ■ Team opportunities

- ■ Sabbaticals

- ■ A variety of training programs and other educational programs

■ **Provide social opportunities.** All work and no play makes work a dull grind. I know executives who frown on mixing work and personal relationships. They believe that personal life should be separate, never introducing their colleagues to family members or inviting them to their homes. Similarly, there are companies that rarely if ever sponsor any employee gatherings that don't relate to business; they don't have company picnics, holiday parties, and the like.

A sense of play is important for the emotional health of all employees. From CEOs on down, there has to be a fun aspect to a job. This doesn't mean that goofing around is encouraged or that having fun becomes the top priority. But a lot of work involves repeated tasks, and routines can become dull. Ideally, people will find a significant amount of fun and satisfaction in the work itself, but that is usually insufficient. Even executives in top positions need relief from the pressure they feel and their routines.

People feel better about working for companies when they think of their colleagues as business friends. Organizations that throw parties to celebrate accomplishments, that designate certain days as ones where people can bring their kids to the office, and that informally encourage friendships among employees are generally those where people trust each other.

▨ **Make laughter a part of the culture.** Admittedly, this last one is tough to establish in any formal way. You can't *demand* people get a sense of humor. Leaders in organizations, however, can model behaviors that communicate it's okay to laugh at yourself; they can joke around and smile a little more often.

Stone-faced CEOs drain the humor out of organizations. In their presence, it feels like a sin to smile, as if you're not taking your work seriously. In ultraserious cultures, mistakes are not forgiven and people don't extend kindness to others. In these companies, people are more likely to cover up a mistake than deal with it honestly and openly.

Leaders, therefore, need to laugh at their own mistakes occasionally. They need to be self-deprecating at times and relieve the pressure of a tense meeting with a joke. When they act this way, others will feel free to loosen up and help foster a more relaxed atmosphere.

A Humanistic External Approach

When you create a culture where relationships, humor, and flexibility are valued, you stand a much better chance of creating a company that stakeholders trust. Employees who are happier, more satisfied in their work, and allowed to be themselves are much more likely to communicate honestly and respectfully with others.

At the same time, it's important to be humanistic externally as well as internally. Too often, people don't treat vendors, partners, and other groups with the same degree of kindness and consideration with which they treat customers. No doubt, you've experienced a company spokesman who deliberately deceived a reporter or someone in a leadership position who manipulated an alliance partner into taking an action it really didn't want to take.

Normally, most employees don't act this way in their personal lives. They're genuine, caring people who don't make it a practice to deceive a friend or lie to a loved one. Yet when they're in a business situation, they rationalize their behavior; they believe the ends of business justify the means. When a significant percentage of a company's employees feel this way, distrust is created.

Although an organization can't control or monitor all its internal-external interactions, it can establish some humanistic guidelines. These guidelines can be communicated in all sorts of ways—memos, role-playing exercises, and so on. The key is to help employees understand that they need to treat a stakeholder with the same consideration that they would extend to anyone who is valued in their lives. Here are some guidelines to help make this point:

■ **Be authentic.** In other words, share who you really are with others, no matter if they're customers or suppliers. Too often, people strike a pose in business situations. They behave in a warm, friendly way when dealing with customers and cold and demanding when dealing with vendors. Artificial personalities are dehumanizing. Other people sense that you're playing a role and it's off-putting. As a result, no real relationship forms, preventing trust from being created.

Jack, a bright and talented marketing director for a large corporation, assumed a slick, hip persona when working with account people at his company's advertising, public relations, and sales promotion agencies. No doubt, he thought that he would fit in better with his contacts at these agencies, many of whom were younger than he was. In fact, the agency people viewed his act as an act. Behind his back, they made fun of his use of supposedly hip expressions. They figured Jack was a phony, making it difficult for them to form a solid relationship with him. They figured that if he would pretend to be someone he was not, they couldn't trust him to be honest about work issues.

In any large organization, there are always going to be people like Jack. Ideally, though, these people will be a distinct minority. A company that hires and promotes people in part because they're willing to be themselves will staff key positions with individuals who are more likely to build trust with stakeholders.

■ **Don't be a bully.** Companies should do a better job monitoring their people for bullying behavior. Managers often treat vendors/suppliers, the media, and other groups with condescension and even hostility. It's almost as if they feel it's their *right* as the buyers of products and services or as the purveyors of information. I've seen numerous examples of executives who don't just push their own people around but who exhibit these same obnoxious behaviors with external contacts.

No one trusts bullies. People may tolerate them because they have to, but they don't like or respect them. No one helps a bully when he's down or extends him the benefit of the doubt. They won't feel any sympathy if the bully's company gets in trouble and needs assistance. Secretly, people are glad when bullying companies get their comeuppance. When they've been treated like ninety-eight-pound weaklings for years, they're happy to see the bully treated the same way.

I've seen some media people exact revenge when an arrogant company seeks them out because it needs something, even though the company has "stiffed" reporters over the years when they requested information and interviews. When these arrogant companies finally need a favor from a reporter, they find that the reporter isn't interested in granting it.

■ **Extend empathy.** Customer service representatives respond brusquely to callers who have complaints about products or services. Leaders have difficulty understanding why a local community or activist group is up in arms over something the company has done. Communications directors find the media's willingness to run an unsubstantiated story about the company to be irresponsible.

Organizations are no longer islands. In this interconnected world, employees can't take an us-versus-them stance. Even though an external group's goals and methods are different from its own, management must communicate to all levels and types of employees that they should try and extend empathy beyond the office walls. Just as companies have diversity training internally, they need external programs as well. Many employees harbor cynical views of customers, reporters, activists, and financial analysts. They see them as "different," as having agendas that conflict with those of their companies.

Empathy is often a precursor to trust. When you demonstrate to people that you understand where they're coming from both in word and deed, they are much more likely to trust you. Of course, some individuals and organizations don't deserve empathy; they may be making unreasonable demands or have a completely selfish agenda. But companies at least have to allow for the possibility of empathy. Too often, it's not even a consideration, and stakeholders are uniformly viewed as a pain in the butt.

▓ **Don't be indifferent/apathetic.** In other words, don't give people the cold shoulder. Instead of hostility, callers or visitors to a company are greeted with boredom. This indifference is almost as bad as negative emotions. It communicates that "you're beneath notice." Everyone has gone to a store and encountered a sales clerk who acts if she couldn't care whether you lived or died. Other forms of apathy, however, are apparent in various organization-stakeholder encounters. Calls aren't returned or are returned only after three or four voice mail messages are left. E-mails are ignored. Meetings are hurried and end abruptly. Conversations lack any enthusiasm.

People who act indifferently toward various groups don't feel they're doing anything wrong; they justify their behaviors as "professional and businesslike." The problem, of course, is that they're communicating an unprofessional, unbusinesslike message: "You don't matter." They possess what therapists refer to as a "flat affect," and it rubs people the wrong way.

The Most Human of Companies

In June 2002, *Crain's* "Chicago Business Survey" identified Deere & Company as Illinois's most-trusted corporation. Its chairman and CEO, Robert W. Lane, has helped Deere maintain its humanistic culture, a culture that started being developed in 1837 when John Deere said, "I will never put my name on a product that does not have in it the best that is in me." Like Ralph Larsen of Johnson & Johnson, Lane spends much of his time communicating, to ensure that everyone understands how much he values ethical, compassionate behavior.

When I talked with him recently, he said that when he joined Deere twenty-one years ago, he was attracted to its 165-year culture of doing things right and its culture of trust. He noted that people who join Deere from other cultures sometimes have a challenging adjustment because "if you work for Deere, we expect you to live up to its principles."

In a speech Lane gave in 2000, he summed up these principles as follows: "While our competitors have merged, consolidated, or otherwise regrouped—each time creating an identity crisis among their products and uncertainty among their customers—John Deere has remained unchanged, holding fast to its time-honored values of quality, integrity, innovation, and commitment."

These aren't just nice-sounding words. During the Depression, Deere didn't demand payment from customers who were far behind on their farm-machinery debts. This was an extraordinary act of generosity at a time when most companies were demanding payment. In the summer of 2002, this scenario repeated itself. It was a difficult year for many farmers because of severe drought conditions, and a significant number were unable to make payments to Deere because of these conditions. Instead of demanding payment, John Deere Credit sent letters to twenty-four thousand customers who had payments coming due, telling them it would find a way to help them through this challenging period.

It's no wonder that Lane is extraordinarily proud of the sizable number of long-term relationships Deere has with customers. Generosity may be its own reward, but it also rewards Deere with the type of mutually beneficial customer relationships other companies can only dream about.

CHAPTER 7

Humility: Developing a Nonarrogant Attitude

A life spent making mistakes is not only more honorable but more useful than a life spent doing nothing.

—GEORGE BERNARD SHAW

Being humble in the face of significant success is a trick many organizations haven't mastered. Too often, they assume that success gives them the right to affect a superior attitude. You've probably worked with organizations where their people responded to your requests and questions with a know-it-all's condescension. From their CEO's speeches to their customer service representatives' responses, they communicate the belief that they are operating at a higher level than everyone else.

These companies mistake arrogance for confidence. It's fine to project an attitude of certainty of purpose and pride in accomplishment. This type of confidence isn't offensive. It doesn't put other people down or suggest that the rules don't apply to them. What happens, though, is that success often goes to people's heads. They develop an unrealistic belief in their infallibility. Typically, this belief starts at the leadership level and seeps its way down through the rest of the company. It results in all sorts of behaviors that range from mildly to extremely offensive. It may be a superior tone of voice, the arrogance of unreturned phone calls, an advertising campaign that is boastful, or an attitude of, "You're lucky to be working with a company like ours."

In these instances, trust is difficult to develop. It's tough to warm up to an arrogant individual; there doesn't seem to be the possibility of a reciprocal, one-on-one relationship. Arrogant organizations communicate a sense of one-upmanship. They don't make the people they do business with feel good about themselves. More than that, they imply that they should have more privileges and leeway than others because they're the best. This attitude creates tremendous resentment.

Humility is a trust-building option, and it's one that some of the world's most successful organizations have embraced.

Humility Doesn't Mean Passive or Weak Willed

Over the years, McDonald's has managed to exhibit great humility in the face of great success. This is due in part to the legacy of Ray Kroc, a business leader who was never above talking to maintenance people and cabbies the same way he talked to other business executives. He clearly communicated his belief that he was no better than anyone else, and he embedded this belief in McDonald's culture. To this day, arrogant individuals don't last long at the company. Either they adjust their attitudes or the culture eventually makes them feel like they're outsiders because of the way they treat others.

Strong leaders of companies can be proud and committed and don't have to constantly remind everyone that their company is far and away the leader in its industry. Perhaps you recall the expression, "If you've got it, flaunt it." I'd change that to "If you've got it, you don't *need* to flaunt it."

Years ago when I worked for MGM, I picked up Clark Gable

and a number of lesser stars at the train station (yes, people were taking lots of trains in those days), and fans were mobbing them, asking for autographs. A little while later, one of the people with us—a minor actress—turned to Gable and said, "Isn't it terrible what we have to go through." Gable said to her, "Honey, when they *stop* bothering me, *that's* when I get worried. It's a small price to pay." For a superstar actor, Gable was amazingly humble. He managed to be down-to-earth despite his fame, and that humility helped endear him to his fans.

Despite this, many business leaders choose to be more like the minor actress than Gable. Because of this choice, they influence their organizations to act like royalty rather than the common man. Certainly organizations don't consciously attempt to project a superior image. Instead, they tell themselves that it's important that they let everyone know they have the best products, the best service, the best prices. Their advertising, their public relations programs, and their relationships with various external groups all reflect this "We're the best" attitude.

Although it's great to be proud of being a market leader and having superior products and services, it's easy to cross the line from pride to arrogance. Companies become so caught up in their success that they commit "sins of pride." See if any of the following sins apply to your organization:

- Treating vendors as if they're lucky to be doing business with your organization

- Running advertising that denigrates competitors as "inferior"

- Refusing reporters' requests for interviews or information

- Creating an internal hierarchy where managers are treated like kings and lower-level employees are treated like serfs

■ Knowingly structuring win-lose deals (where your company makes out great and your partner gets the short end of the stick)

■ Using your clout and leadership position to push people around (such as the media, suppliers, etc.)

■ Giving top executives large bonuses during tough times (after a year of layoffs and lower revenues)

■ Ignoring industry concerns because you feel they don't apply to a market leader such as your company

■ Not taking customer complaints seriously, assuming that the problem lies with them and not you

■ Telling financial analysts that you're expecting a great year even though you sincerely doubt that will be the case

■ Creating "snobby" hiring practices that screen out job candidates who didn't go to the best business schools, work in the top organizations or consulting firms, and otherwise lack the right pedigree

■ Building a culture where anyone who challenges the company's traditions or practices is criticized and ostracized

Every organization commits some of these sins some of the time. The problem is when they become standard operating procedure. When an arrogant attitude becomes widespread and deep-rooted, then it produces even more egregious sins. Think about some of the recent scandals that created great distrust and how arrogance was at their root. Specifically:

■ Former Tyco CEO Dennis Kozlowski spent enormous sums of money on homes, yachts, and other purchases, allegedly using corporate funds to finance some of these expenditures. It can be reasonably argued that his arrogance—his belief that he was above the rules that govern the behavior of other CEOs—allowed him to spend money in this manner.

■ WorldCom executives reportedly inflated profits by placing $3.8 billion in expenses on the plus side of the ledger. It's difficult to imagine how they thought they could get away with this alleged chicanery unless they believed they were too clever to get caught.

■ ImClone CEO Sam Waksal allegedly tipped friends off to sell their ImClone stock right before regulators rejected ImClone's application for a new drug, and he was indicted for insider trading. Again, if these charges are correct, then Waksal must have realized that what he was doing was both unethical and illegal, but he also must have felt he possessed some sort of immunity, that the government couldn't touch him.

Though arrogance doesn't always result in these catastrophic or illegal acts, it does help people justify actions that can't be justified. It warps people's perspectives, allowing them to believe that what's wrong is right. As a result, they say and do things that create distrust.

Why Arrogance Is Such an Enticing Trap

After all of the financial scandals, you would think that business leaders would know better, that they would realize arrogance breeds distrust. Even without the financial scandals, you would assume that they would realize how off-putting a superior attitude can be.

Unfortunately, a number of factors *blind* people to the negative impact of arrogance. First, many leaders believe their own publicity. In recent years, top business executives like Jack Welch and Louis Gerstner have become superstars. They've been on magazine covers, written best-selling books, and appeared on talk shows. Their companies provide them with private jets and many other amenities formerly reserved for world leaders. They're paid princely sums and enjoy a lavish lifestyle. Many of these CEOs think they can do no wrong because of the avalanche of input suggesting exactly that. It's very difficult for them to step back and realize that their self-image is distorted. They don't see their flaws, and consequently they start *acting* like superstars. To a certain extent, this isn't their fault. They're just fulfilling other people's expectations of them. There's no question that Jack Welch is a brilliant leader, but he's not as brilliant as he or others thought he was. With hindsight, we can see that he made some poor acquisitions, bullied direct reports, and abused his position in other ways. Arrogance robbed him of foresight. I'm sure that to Jack Welch, his attitude and privileges seemed his due as a great leader.

Second, CEOs have gotten into the habit of surrounding themselves with people who think like they do. At one very successful dot-com company, the twenty-nine-year-old founder and president had five vice presidents who reported to him. All were male, all were in their twenties, and all had similar backgrounds (computer science majors, etc.). Consensus was easily achieved among this group, and they joked that they knew each other so well they could read each other's minds. When the dot-com shakeout occurred, this company was one of the first casualties, and the CEO was shocked that its fortunes had reversed so quickly. He had arrogantly created a lot of debt for the firm, spending freely on technology and salaries, assuming that this debt would all be taken care of when it had its initial public offering. Unfortunately, the company waited too long and the offering was a dismal failure. The CEO couldn't imagine the dot-com boom ever going bust and neither could his direct reports. No one ever challenged the CEO's viewpoint, allowing his arrogance to remain intact.

Of course, it's not just young high-tech pioneers who commit this sin. Even veteran CEOs have a tendency to surround themselves with people they have worked with over the years, individuals whom they've gone to battle with and trust. Ironically, these trusted coworkers ultimately produce distrust because they are unable or unwilling to provide the CEO with fresh ideas and challenging perspectives. The CEO, pleased with consistent consensus, firmly believes his ideas are right and refuses to consider other points of view. He is absolutely bullish about his programs and strategies, convinced that if they weren't right, a member of his inner circle would have informed him of such. This CEO, therefore, doesn't *believe* he's arrogant. Instead, he's absolutely convinced that he is right and that it would be a waste of time to consider other opinions or do additional research.

Third, boards have allowed CEO arrogance to rage out of control. Although a board of directors may not be specifically charged with keeping a CEO's ego in check, it is an implicit part of their governance role when his ego is hurting the organization. Especially in this day and age, boards should make it their business to ensure the CEO is not creating distrust. When they see that a CEO is insular, proud to the point of hubris, and unwilling to listen to dissenting opinions, they need to take action. The reality, however, is that boards often don't do anything. In part, this is because of the cozy relationship that often exists between boards and CEOs. They're members of the same club reserved for highly successful business leaders. Because they have a type of gentleman's agreement, they condone arrogant behaviors that alienate employees and other stakeholders. Not only should boards be calling these CEOs on the carpet, but they should be screening candidates in order to red flag this trait in the CEO selection process.

Fourth, in uncertain, unpredictable times, arrogance is a defense mechanism. It's very difficult for smart, successful leaders to face up to the fact that their strategies aren't working or that they've made mistakes. Some of them seek refuge in arrogance, convincing both themselves and others that they know exactly what they're doing. It's threatening to admit that they aren't sure or they have made an error. Many CEOs were trained to believe that they should never show weakness or admit uncertainty. As a result, they wear their arrogance as a shield, especially if things aren't going well for the company.

Fifth, many CEOs and other executives—especially the younger ones—have never experienced hard times. Consequently, they can't envision anything but success, and this reinforces their excessive pride and ego. Years ago, people rarely rose to management level without paying their dues and experiencing some type of failure along the way. Today, people with extraordinary skills are promoted quickly, and they may not have much chance to have learned from their mistakes. This is not to say that we should *avoid* putting younger leaders in positions of responsibility, only that we should recognize that some of them may have had a smooth sail to the top, and it's very difficult to be humble when nothing has ever humbled you.

How to Create Humility

A little humility can go a long way in building trust. It's not enough that just one department or group is self-effacing. There are companies where one department is known for being gracious, modest, and a pleasure to deal with, and another department has a reputation for being snobbish boors who are constantly issuing orders and failing to listen. This split personality does not create trust. Instead, the trusted company is one where customer service representatives never talk down to customers, no matter how basic their questions are; where people routinely return calls quickly and politely; where leaders have open door policies and don't use positional power to get things done (preferring to use influence instead); and where vendors are treated as partners rather than order takers. In other words, humility is built into the culture, a natural way of acting that is embraced by the majority of employees.

How do you decrease the overall arrogance and increase the overall humility of your organization? Here are four steps you can take:

1. Monitor arrogant hot spots. The odds are that you know at least some people in your company who adopt arrogant attitudes when dealing with customers, employees, and others. You know a corporate communications vice president who consistently treats reporters like second-class citizens or a manager who favors commands rather than requests when he needs direct reports to take on a task. Many times, these people aren't even conscious of their arrogance. They may be good candidates for coaching. A good coach can often motivate managers to moderate their arrogance, helping them become aware of how their behavior has hurt the people they work with as well as their own careers.

Other people, of course, will be more resistant to efforts aimed at moderating their arrogance. Some may require coaching interventions. There are those individuals, though, who are arrogant to the core, and I wouldn't want these people working for me. I also don't enjoy working with such individuals. One of our client companies was headed by a smart and successful CEO— we'll call him Martin. He perceived himself to be smarter and more successful than anyone else and wasn't shy about sharing this perception with others. One day we had lunch, and prior to our lunch one of Martin's direct reports let me know that he might not be in a particularly good mood because he had just terminated a number of people in his company. At lunch, I mentioned that I heard about the downsizing and said that he must not be feeling too good about it.

Martin told me he was actually feeling quite good because most companies let go of people when a company isn't doing well, but he was letting go of people when his company was doing great. It almost seemed as if he enjoyed firing them; that he felt he was smarter than other CEOs because he was getting rid of employees sooner rather than later.

Martin is the sort of person *I* would get rid of sooner rather than later. As CEO, he sets an example that encourages other people in the company to act like they are infallible, not to mention intimidating.

Monitoring the organization for arrogance doesn't have to be an overly formal or intrusive process. The goal isn't to listen in on conversations or turn everyone into Mother Teresa. Nor is the goal to eliminate all superior attitudes or overconfident behavior—everyone is going to have moments when they are boastful, demanding, or pedantic. The purpose of monitoring is simply to get runaway arrogance under control. When it's "managed," trust is easier to create.

2. Educate people about the difference between arrogance and pride. This concept needs to be integrated into an organization's management and leadership training. People mistakenly believe that if they're working for a market leader or if their company has been successful, they've earned the right to act like they're the best. They're tremendously proud of what their organizations have accomplished and feel entitled to show their pride. Although being proud of a company's accomplishments is great, people cross the line when they become obnoxiously proud. Using a company's prestige and success to beat up other people by telling them they don't measure up to "our" standards is pure arrogance. Feeling that you don't have to respond to probing questions from the media or financial analysts because of your leadership position—you're above all that—is another form of arrogance.

Training and development programs need to communicate that there's nothing soft or weak about humility; that in fact, it takes great strength as a leader to tamp down one's ego and treat people fairly and equally. Perhaps the best way to do this is by making a clear distinction between *arrogance* and *pride,* the latter of which is quite compatible with humility. To that end, here are some common examples of the differences between these two concepts:

A: Expecting unquestioning obedience

P: Expecting respectful challenges

A: Issuing orders

P: Making requests

A: Boasting about the company's greatness

P: Making specific references to the company's accomplishments

A: Rejecting ideas that aren't aligned with the company's tradition or strategy

P: Rejecting ideas after careful analysis because they don't meet the company's goals

A: Creating an inner circle that keeps most people out

P: Creating a flexible circle that encompasses a diversity of expert opinion

A: Demanding that people do it your way

P: Expecting people to consider your way

A: Believing that your organization can do no wrong

P: Believing in the strengths of your organization while being aware of its weaknesses

A: Refusing to acknowledge a mistake

P: Acknowledging mistakes but being able to recover from them quickly and with confidence

3. Use advertising and public relations to communicate a company's humility. Some companies value humility yet they don't let anyone know it. They make little or no effort to tell the world that this is a corporate value and that they live this value in a hundred different ways. I've known organizations that had reputations for arrogance that in fact were not arrogant at all. Their reputations were based on old news—former CEOs were arrogant or one incident created a false impression in the minds of the public. Perception sometimes counts more than reality, and people can distrust companies that *seem* arrogant as much as they do companies that *are* arrogant.

It's not always easy to create awareness that your company is down-to-earth and that it treats people fairly. People who try and project this humble image can come off as self-serving and insincere. There was a CEO who was known for being insular and elitist, but he became enamored of the "management by walking around" philosophy. He decided that he would spend one day on the factory floor, shaking hands with employees and attempting to work on the assembly line. A photographer took shots of the CEO working on the line, but they were never sent to the media because the CEO looked so uncomfortable and out of place that if they had been sent, everyone would have realized this was a token gesture.

On the other hand, a large direct marketing company did a great job of projecting an image of equality and fairness when it generated numerous stories about its open office design. The CEO at the time had transformed the company, and as part of the transformation he had done away with all offices, including his own. Everyone worked in open spaces in order to facilitate better communication among different groups and to create a more egalitarian atmosphere. The media picked up on this story, and the publicity greatly helped the company with recruiting and re-tention.

Some organizations have done a great job of projecting a humble image through advertising. Though they've achieved this goal in many different ways, one of the most effective seems to be by poking gentle fun at themselves. For years, Volkswagen ran ads with a "Think Small" theme that turned a weakness into a strength—it made fun of the car's size and somewhat unattractive shape, endearing the company to millions of people. The late Dave Thomas of Wendy's appeared as the spokesperson in his commercials. Rather than position himself as a wise and authoritative chairman, he communicated that he was an ordinary guy and a bit of bumbler. We thought of him as our favorite uncle or neighbor. Everyone could identify with him because he was so approachable and likable, and he sold a lot of hamburgers as a result.

4. Study history. As the saying goes, people who don't know history are condemned to repeat it. Organizations and their leaders would be less arrogant if they were aware of how quickly and precipitously other companies and their CEOs have fallen. Until relatively recently, no one ever said a negative word about Jack

Welch. Enron and WorldCom were considered superstar corporations that could do no wrong. Record companies that experienced a rebirth with the advent of compact discs are now struggling (in part because they arrogantly refused to lower CD prices even though many record companies assured the public that they would indeed come down as the technology became more popular).

A historically astute management team knows the perils of assuming success can be sustained indefinitely. At the very least, companies should make an effort to make their people aware of their company's history as well as of other companies in their industry. Invariably, a cyclical pattern of success and failure emerges. Even if a company has dominated its industry, it too has had its ups and downs. Being able to look at your current situation within a historical perspective tends to *diminish* arrogance. The one consistent lesson history teaches is that *nothing* lasts forever.

Moderation Is the Goal

You're never going to get rid of all the arrogant people, attitudes, and behaviors in your company. There are also times when bluster is called for. In certain situations, you need to match a reporter's or competitor's arrogance with your own.

The modest goal here is moderation. If you can help people become more aware of the distrust-building effects of arrogance and of their own tendencies to display arrogance, you'll help moderate the negative impact. At heart, most people are decent individuals who don't want to be perceived as snobs or jerks. If you can foster awareness of this issue in the various ways discussed here, at least some of the people in your company will self-regulate their arrogance. If this happens, you'll see a subtle but meaningful impact on both internal and external relationships. Salespeople will treat customers with a little more consideration. Managers will be less likely to push around direct reports. Top executives will be more willing to *communicate* rather than lecture.

If these small shifts occur, your company will have incrementally reduced one significant barrier to creating trust.

CHAPTER 8

Speed, Truth, and Other Good Ways to Respond to Bad Times

Always do right; this will gratify some people and astonish the rest.

—MARK TWAIN

C rises are when companies are most likely to create distrust. Under stress, in the spotlight, and dealing with sensitive issues, management often says and does things that alienate a significant audience. This isn't the intent, but it's often the result, especially when management has failed to create a trust bank that can mitigate the negative impact of these situations.

I'm defining crisis broadly here. To give you a sense of the range of crises that can create distrust, here are just some examples:

- Downsizing
- Labor unrest (strikes)
- Product safety problem
- Product quality issue
- Negative media publicity (relating to any of the other crisis topics)

- Discrimination lawsuit

- Government regulatory charges against company

- Accusations of financial shenanigans

- A poor quarter or year

- Environmental problems (e.g., activist group charges that the company is polluting land, air, or water)

- Problems with community groups

- Service snafus

None of these events or problems *has* to become a full-blown crisis. There are instances when a strike is settled quickly and amicably or when product quality problems don't amount to much. Nonetheless, they all have the potential to escalate into a crisis, and when that happens, distrust can spread with startling speed.

Sugar Is Not Always Sweet: How One Company Dealt with a Distasteful Problem

In 1996, the Center for Science in the Public Interest (CSPI) attacked Gerber for adding starch and sugar to its baby food products. CSPI, a consumer watchdog group for the food industry, leveled its charges at the worst possible time: Gerber had recently begun losing market share to Beechnut and other competitors. The media found the story irresistible, in part because Gerber was the market leader and had enjoyed a squeaky clean image for many years.

Over the years, Gerber had made many deposits into its trust bank. From the well-known logo of a baby on its products, to its commitment to quality ingredients, to its efforts to fight diseases like Sudden Infant Death Syndrome, Gerber had worked hard to become a trusted brand. Suddenly, though, everything had changed. The CSPI's charges carried the clear implication that Gerber was more concerned with profit than products, that it was ignoring the data about what constituted healthy food for infants.

Despite the negative publicity and declining market share, Gerber *didn't* panic. It *didn't* lash out at the CSPI and claim it was being victimized. It *didn't* offer excuses. It *didn't* close its eyes and hope all the fuss would die down. Instead, Gerber launched a carefully considered plan to regain and build trust. At the heart of the plan was the introduction of a new line of products that included a brand extension called Gerber Wellness; it also removed much of the starch and sugar from its products. But Gerber made sure that the announcement of these changes didn't appear to be a knee-jerk response to negative publicity (which it wasn't— Gerber had been working on formulating new products before CSPI issued its statement). Gerber acknowledged that it intended to make changes, but it did so in a carefully orchestrated manner. For instance, part of the message that Gerber conveyed through its advertising and public relations efforts was that it was willing to take heat from advocacy groups and would not be rushed into bringing new products to market until they had the correct recipes. It also reinforced the message that for seventy years, Gerber had been the number one choice of parents, and that it had established a tradition of quality and caring that it intended to maintain. In addition, Gerber emphasized its commitment to charitable, child-related causes. And finally, it turned negative publicity into positive by taking advantage of the spotlight, drawing greater attention to the new line of organic products than it ordinarily would have received.

In a relatively short period of time, Gerber had not only rebuilt whatever trust it had lost but strengthened the bonds of trust with customers and other stakeholders. In 1998, Gerber received top scores in a customer brand loyalty study. The company's market share rose to 70 percent after having fallen to the low 60s. And CSPI, the organization that leveled the charges initially, recognized Gerber with its Chairman's Commendation Award and membership in the "Safety Circle" program.

What Not to Do: The Biggest Mistakes Companies Make

We've learned a number of do's and don'ts from our work with Gerber and other companies facing crisis situations. First, let's look at the following don'ts:

■ **Don't act like a victim.** More than one company has responded to a crisis with a victim mentality. The CEO appears and protests that the company is the victim of circumstance, such as a downturn in the economy. Or she attributes the problem to someone else's mistake: A supplier provided the company with faulty products. Whether or not this is true is irrelevant. The real victims are the people who were harmed by bad products, by being downsized, by a sudden drop in the company's stock price. They don't want to hear the company whining about how it was victimized. Such whining doesn't inspire trust, but the suspicion that it is unwilling to accept responsibility. People don't want to hear excuses or rationales, as valid as they might be. Or rather, they don't want these excuses or rationales to be the first and most significant response to a crisis. When there's an oil spill, they want to hear what the oil company is going to do to clean up the mess. They don't want to hear about how they were victimized by bad weather or a poorly constructed ship. When employees go out on strike, customers who are inconvenienced by the strike don't want to hear how the strikers are at fault because they are making unreasonable demands. They want to know what the company is doing to end the strike and restore customer service to prestrike levels.

■ **Don't close your eyes and hope the problem will go away.** I offer this advice realizing that in a minority of cases, problems do go away. Perhaps one or two times out of every ten, a crisis clears up on its own with little negative fallout. For whatever reason, you don't lose trust because of the crisis. This possibility encourages leaders to think that this is a viable strategy in the face of a crisis, especially when the media is involved. People assume that the media's interest in any story is short-lived, and that if they refuse to comment, the whole thing will blow over within days. Although the media may indeed lose interest in a few days, the repercussions from their stories last a lot longer. When you clam up and refuse to provide any statements or information, the stories can be devastating and create a highly untrustworthy image for a company. In other instances, the media can periodically return to a story and re-create the feelings of distrust that you thought had gone away.

Refusing to respond to employee demands, financial analysts' inquiries, government regulators' requests, customer complaints, and activist boycotts all can make a bad situation worse. It sends a clear and unequivocal message that your company doesn't care. If it cared, it would respond. Silence and inaction often seem like an admission of guilt, the logic being: If you're innocent, you'll want to state your case for the record.

An activist group was protesting one company's poor record in hiring minorities; the protest consisted of pickets in front of the company's headquarters. Because the protesting group was local and not particularly well known or large, management decided to ignore the protest, assuming the group would soon grow tired of standing outside the company's headquarters, especially since winter was approaching. There also wasn't much media coverage of the protesters, which convinced the CEO and his advisers that they shouldn't make a mountain out of a molehill.

The group of ten to fifteen protesters, though, was persistent, showing up every day at 8:30 A.M. Some of these protesters were women with small children, and one day there was a major snowstorm, and the protesters arrived and stayed. Someone alerted the media about a "photo opportunity," and there were pictures of women and kids huddled together against the snow and cold as well-dressed executives hurried past them into the warmth of the building; there were also moving interviews with the out-of-work women. Things snowballed. Other organizations lent their support and soon the number of protesters increased dramatically. After a while, even employees complained to management about its unwillingness to hire more minority workers. An editorial in the local paper condemned the company's hiring policies, and a major business publication ran a similarly uncomplimentary story. By the time the company caved in to the protesters' demands, the trust damage had already been done.

■ **Don't take a Band-Aid approach.** In other words, don't respond to a crisis with a superficial solution. Too often, companies offer offended parties a Band-Aid. They make minor concessions to disgruntled employees or they agree to modify an information system in small ways even though they promised a customer major changes. Although this may buy a company a little bit of trust in the short term, it backfires in the long term. There's nothing worse than giving the appearance of responding to another group's requirements only for it to realize that it was just an appearance. This can ratchet distrust to an even higher level than it would have been if you had just done nothing. Whatever you did to precipitate the crisis, it's often not as harmful as pretending to give people what they asked for when the pretense is exposed.

Don't say you're going to fix things and then fail to act on that promise. There have been numerous instances of CEOs promising financial analysts after a bad quarter that they're going to launch a great new product or service in the coming year that's going to generate tremendous revenues. In addition, some companies have developed terrible reputations among suppliers because they squeeze them for every last dollar and treat them like dirt. When these companies realize that it's tough to find a supplier that wants to work with them, they guarantee that they've changed their operating procedures, that they're going to get rid of their purchasing manager (whom they blame for past problems), or that they will share all financial information with their suppliers. These promises sound great, but when they're not backed up with action, people become tremendously disillusioned with these organizations.

These Band-Aid approaches may not be undertaken with malicious intent. In some instances, companies really believe that their minor concessions are major ones and that these concessions should repair the damage. Or they honestly intend to back up their words with deeds but circumstances prevent them from doing so—they don't have the money or other resources to implement promised changes and programs.

For this reason, don't respond to a crisis by the seat of your pants and make promises you're not sure you can keep.

What to Do: A Trust-Based Approach to Crisis Management

Because crises can vary considerably, any advice about how to deal with them must be taken with a grain of salt. Some crises, for instance, are monumental in their scope and impact. The Tylenol tampering case, United Airlines' financial woes, and AT&T's deregulation are three examples of such a crisis. Because of the magnitude of these problems and because of the intense media coverage, these companies had to respond differently than companies whose problems were more localized and less visible. Similarly, some crises involve unique, industry-specific issues. Pacific Gas and Electric in 2001, for instance, had to order rolling blackouts in California, and many of the issues it faced were clearly unique to that situation.

Therefore, the following suggestions are designed to help you manage a crisis from a trust perspective. Crisis management is a broad topic, and your strategy is going to be dictated by situational factors. Within this strategy, however, you can take six steps that increase your odds of maintaining and building trust, no matter what the crisis involves:

1. Respond quickly. Perhaps this is self-evident. With hindsight and distance from a crisis, you can understand how important it is to act with great speed to address a significant problem. In the heat of battle, though, our thinking sometimes becomes muddled. Advisers give conflicting opinions, the media exerts tremendous pressure, and there's no obvious "right" response. We don't want to make a mistake, and so we may decide to "count to ten" and not take any definitive action immediately. Perhaps we justify this wait-and-see approach by telling ourselves we need to gather more information before making a decision. The problem, of course, is that we appear indecisive and unconcerned about the impact of the crisis.

Acting fast, on the other hand, communicates decisiveness and caring. Even if you can't offer a solution to the problem immediately, you can offer ideas and take a position. Being *visible* and *responsive* is more likely to maintain trust than being invisible and unresponsive. Just as significantly, responding quickly with information related to the crisis helps squelch rumors before they start. Rumors arise when something bad happens and an information vacuum develops. The way to stop these trust-diminishing rumors from surfacing and spreading is to answer questions quickly.

In 1990, AT&T experienced an unprecedented and widespread loss of phone service due to a technician making software changes at the wrong time. AT&T responded by quickly restoring service. Just as important, CEO Robert Allen didn't blame the problem on the software technician. Instead, he told the media that the software problem was his fault and took full responsibility. He also announced that AT&T was giving its callers a free day of service on Valentine's Day to compensate for the glitch. Marilyn Laurie, the former chief of communications at AT&T, was quoted in the *Wall Street Journal* about the philosophy for handling the crisis, and she said, "Tell the truth, tell it fast, take accountability. And give something back."

If AT&T had done exactly what it did at a slower rate, it would not have restored trust as quickly as it restored service. AT&T didn't give people the time to speculate about what caused the problem or to start looking for scapegoats. Allen quickly took responsibility rather than waiting to decide how to handle this issue and allowing internal bickering and finger pointing to surface. As a result, he helped build trust both internally and externally.

2. Tell the responsible truth. *Responsible* is a key modifier. In the previous example, Allen didn't tell the *whole* truth. To do so would have unfairly singled out a technician who made an honest mistake as well as given the appearance that this huge corporation was picking on a powerless employee. Some may argue that you should always tell the complete and unadorned truth, and I would counter their argument with the one I used with my mother. She was guilty of telling the unvarnished truth and frequently got in trouble with relatives because she didn't mince words. Even when I was a teenager, I used to argue with her about this tendency. I'd point to an unattractive person sitting at a nearby table in a restaurant and ask her if she thought it was appropriate to tell this person she was ugly. I couldn't convince her that the whole truth and nothing but was *not* always a good idea, but I hope you'll take this concept to heart, especially in the heat of a crisis.

I'm not advocating lying to shield your company or to manipulate stakeholders. Honesty is crucial, but it needs to be tempered by a realistic assessment of how that honesty will impact others. Consider the following situation. Your company has had a bad year and you're forced to lay off people. Management decides to lay off only 5 percent of the workforce, even though the numbers indicate it should be laying off 10 percent. Management hopes that other cost-cutting measures and an upturn in sales in the coming year will help get the company's revenues up to where they need to be. If they don't, however, another round of layoffs may be necessary. To tell this "truth" to employees, especially, is not the responsible thing to do. It would create unnecessary panic, and some people might seek and accept a less attractive job than the one they currently hold. Certainly employees should be given as much advance warning as possible if another layoff is determined to be necessary, but the negatives of telling them the whole truth outweigh the positives in this instance.

Admittedly, it's not always easy to know if telling the complete truth during a crisis will cause more harm than good. To help you make this determination, ask yourself the following questions:

- If we tell the *whole* truth, what negative impact will it have; what specific individuals or groups will suffer; what form will this suffering take?

- If we don't tell the complete truth, can we avoid the negative reactions previously identified; if so, are there other, even more negative, consequences that could result from being less than completely honest?

- What are the positives of telling the *responsible* truth versus telling the whole truth?

- If you were to compare the negatives and positives of the responsible truth with the whole truth, which option seems to make more sense?

Another way to assess these two types of truths is to look at the impact on all stakeholders. Too often, companies in crisis modes tend to evaluate options based only on self-interest. This may make sense from a financial standpoint, but it's not necessarily a good idea from a trust point of view. Therefore, ask yourself the following question: How would the complete and unvarnished truth impact each of the following groups: employees, financial analysts, customers, suppliers, the community, advocacy groups, government regulatory agencies?

It may be that the whole truth will benefit your various stakeholders and hurt you. Or it's possible that two stakeholder groups will benefit from this truth and one will not. There are lots of possibilities, and I don't have any great wisdom about how to deal with this confusing situation except to advise analyzing the impact on all stakeholders before making a decision. This truth-telling decision should result in either the greatest good for the greatest number of people or the least harm to the fewest people.

In thinking about whether you should tell the whole truth, keep in mind the scene from the movie *A Few Good Men*, where Jack Nicholson, playing a tough marine officer, is mercilessly questioned by Tom Cruise's lawyer character during a court-martial trial, and in response to a request for the truth, Nicholson responds: "You can't *handle* the truth!"

3. Be willing to say, "I don't know." Just as I'd prefer having a doctor who admits he's not sure of what's causing a problem (rather than arrogantly speculating on the cause), I'd rather hear a company say, "I don't know," in response to a crisis than have it adopt a falsely authoritative posture. Again, the machismo of some corporate leaders is such that they feel compelled to provide answers in the wake of a crisis, even when they're not sure what these answers are. For instance, a food company finds that some of its canned goods are contaminated by illness-causing bacteria, and the CEO immediately makes an announcement that the company knows the cause of the problem, that it's limited to a very small batch of product, and that it has already implemented steps that will ensure it won't happen again. In fact, it knows none of these things. It may have its suspicions and can make some pretty good guesses, but it's too early to know anything definitive. Nonetheless, the CEO feels the need to act like he's in control of the situation. The cost of control, however, may be that more people consume tainted products.

The ideal trust-building response in these situations is to say "I don't know," when you really don't know, but to provide as much information as possible to limit the rumors and panic that can surface in the absence of definitive explanations. Saying you don't know will not be perceived as a sign of ignorance or weakness if other, helpful information is provided. In most cases, people respect business leaders who are brave enough to admit they don't have all the answers. Of course, it helps enormously if these leaders provide people with information about what they're doing to get these answers. If the company's stock is going down and there's no clear cause for the drop, the company spokesperson can express her uncertainty as to the cause but should also discuss the analysis the company is undertaking in order to pinpoint the problems and the steps it's taking to reverse this trend.

Think about it from a personal level. I don't know about you, but I respect my doctor more when he doesn't give me a pat answer to one of my questions and is willing to admit he doesn't know the answer.

4. Have empathy and show compassion. This doesn't mean feel sorry for yourself. Although crises negatively impact the leaders of an organization, they often have a much greater negative impact on customers, rank-and-file employees, shareholders, and so on. It's great if you can take specific actions to moderate the negative impact, but it's just as important to be compassionate toward the people who have been hurt. Whether it's downsized employees, customers who haven't received their products, or shareholders whose stock in your company has lost value, you should clearly communicate you appreciate what they're going through.

This is more than lip service. It requires that corporate executives take the time to talk to people who have been adversely affected. It requires that executives also take the time to reflect on what these people tell them, consider the corporation's responsibility, and try and feel what these people are feeling. It is the humanistic thing to do, and it is what allows you to have empathy and show compassion. A compassionate response is much more likely to earn the company trust than neutrality or, even worse, feigned sympathy.

Unfortunately, many organizational leaders don't always exhibit empathy during crises. They're cool and objective, which may facilitate decision making but doesn't help build trust. After some sort of major snafu or disaster, people want to believe that the company that helped precipitate a crisis (or that seems in some way responsible for it) understands their plight. Some executives, though, not only fail to display compassion but inadvertently display contempt.

Even smart, trust-building leaders can commit this sin. Earlier, we talked about how former AT&T CEO Robert Allen earned trust internally and externally by taking responsibility for a service problem. Five years later, though, AT&T laid off forty thousand employees. AT&T's Marilyn Laurie noted in a speech given to the

Arthur Page Society in 2002 that "the sheer magnitude of that number . . . was perceived as the deathblow to lifetime employment among large companies in America. Our employees were in an uproar and morale was terrible." A month later, AT&T's board gave Allen a significant raise and bonus.

5. Take preventative action. In other words, do what is necessary to prevent a recurrence of the crisis. This may seem obvious, but in many situations, no preventative measures are taken. In some instances, companies assume that a crisis is a once-in-a-lifetime occurrence. In other instances, they believe there's nothing they can do to prevent a similar crisis from recurring. As a result, they sit on their hands, and this sends a message that the company isn't particularly concerned about the crisis.

When people died from cyanide-laced Tylenol, Johnson & Johnson took the extraordinary preventative measure of creating tamper-proof caps. When AT&T experienced a number of service outages in the 1990s, it spent a great deal of time and money updating equipment to ensure that these major outages wouldn't recur. These measures were very effective, but even if you can't take equally effective measures, you can do something after a crisis to demonstrate you're doing everything possible to prevent a recurrence. If you have just downsized your workforce, this may mean cutting costs from top to bottom—limiting the amount spent on expense account meals, freezing executive bonuses and raises, etc. If you just had an accounting scandal, this may mean setting up an independent oversight committee to monitor accounting procedures.

It's also important to take these preventative measures as soon as possible after a crisis and to *communicate* to relevant groups exactly what you're doing. In terms of the former point, you want to demonstrate that you're taking action while the "hurt is hot." It's difficult to dilute distrust caused by a crisis when the memory of the crisis is clear but the emotion of it has faded. In other words, you have to reach people when their anger and disappointment are fresh; it's this emotion that's at the core of distrust. In addition, you must communicate the basic facts of your preventative measures. You don't need to do anything fancy; you don't want to use hyperbole or pat yourself on the back. But you do want to make sure that appropriate audiences are aware that you're doing something. This can be as simple as a memo to employees or a press release to the media, as long as it gets the message across clearly and quickly to the right people.

6. Compensate appropriately. Sometimes there's no way to provide adequate compensation. How do you compensate shareholders when the stock price plummets or an activist group that accuses the company (unfairly, you believe) of discrimination? In many cases, though, a company can compensate people with money, products, and services for the problems they suffered. Compensation for downsized workers may mean a fair severance payment and outplacement services. Compensation for company-caused pollution may involve clean-up efforts. Compensation for defective products may include free replacements.

The key is to respond in a fair and fiscally responsible manner. There are times when companies simply don't have the financial resources necessary to pay back stakeholders who have suffered because of their errors. There are also instances where companies honestly believe that they're not at fault for a crisis and are certain that no one expects them to compensate aggrieved parties for the totality of their losses. Compensation can be a highly subjective issue—especially when the legal system is involved—and though companies should err on the side of generosity, they should not endanger the fiscal health of their organizations. It does no one any good if a company downsizes thousands of workers, provides them with incredible severance deals, and then has to downsize even more people because they were overly generous with severance.

Putting the Pedal to the Metal to Get Through a Crisis

Hyundai Motor America had successfully made the transition from a company known for its "cheap" automobiles to one recognized as a value brand when a potential disaster struck. In 2002, Hyundai learned that its horsepower data had been misstated in marketing materials for more than ten years. These misstatements impacted 1.5 million vehicles, and it threatened the quality reputation that it had worked long and hard to build. Hyundai created a plan to deal with this crisis.

In terms of the trust-building crisis tactics, Hyundai was especially good at compensating appropriately, telling the responsible truth, and taking preventative measures. Based on research and focus groups, Hyundai determined that though the misstatements had no impact on automobile safety or reliability and weren't intended to mislead customers, it needed to compensate customers for the error. Astutely, Hyundai conducted research and learned that customers valued warranties more than horsepower. As a result, Hyundai offered customers warranty enhancements, compensation that was perceived by customers as more than fair. Just as significantly, the company used its CEO, Finbarr O'Neill, as the spokesperson on this issue initially. His participation demonstrated that Hyundai was taking the matter seriously. He also was a terrific spokesperson who effectively communicated the steps the company was taking to ensure that misstatements didn't happen again.

Hyundai also did an excellent job of telling the appropriate truth to a number of different audiences. Though Hyundai owners and lessees were the primary audience, the company wanted to reach the automotive media, their dealers, and their employees with the facts about what took place. Through an all-day news conference, the Hyundai Web site, information packets, letters, and e-mails, Hyundai communicated exactly what each group needed to know. To make sure all the facts were communicated to customers, Hyundai set up call centers where customers could ask trained operators whatever questions they had about the mileage overstatement, warranty enhancements, and other issues.

Trust was maintained because of these efforts. After the crisis, vehicle sales continued to soar; the following month set a record for sales. Just as significantly, Hyundai received praise from various audiences for how they handled the problem.

CHAPTER 9

Tough Trust Decisions

Well done is better than well said.

—BENJAMIN FRANKLIN

Building and maintaining trust isn't always a black-and-white issue. It can involve a great deal of ambiguity and uncertainty about when and how to take action. Even organizations that have made strong commitments to building trust face gray areas where a number of options will present themselves. Invariably, they will have to make tough decisions about trust bank efforts, responses to crises, and communication strategies.

Although it's difficult to anticipate all the tough trust decisions your organization will encounter, it's worthwhile to consider some of these decisions in advance. You need to be prepared for difficult choices, and the best way to prepare is by rehearsing the process you'll go through to make these choices. For this reason, I've created nine common trust scenarios. Each is based on a composite of real situations that I've observed during my career. More significantly, the scenarios all ask you to contemplate how you might respond if your organization is in a similar situation.

After reading each scenario, don't immediately move on to the next section. Take a moment and reflect on what *your* organization would do if faced with the same options confronting the company in the scenario. After this reflection, you'll better appreciate the analysis of the right and wrong things to do.

SCENARIO 1.

Danilus Inc. has ten plants located in the United States, and it has experienced labor problems in recent years. Two years ago workers at one of its plants went out on strike over a number of issues, including wages they felt were below the norm. Last year, a group of workers at a different plant leaked a story to a reporter about how the company was cutting corners by substituting a lower-cost material in one of its products. A few days ago, regulators shut another Danilus plant down for violating safety regulations. Correcting these violations could take two or three months, and Danilus's management team isn't sure how to deal with the 224 employees of the plant. The CEO is concerned about further negative publicity if Danilus lays off all these workers; he's also worried that if it does lay off employees, some of them will obtain new jobs in the interim and the company will have to go through a time-consuming and costly hiring process to replace them when the plant reopens. Plus, the CEO is certain that this closing is having a negative impact on all Danilus employees, that they feel this is the latest in a series of actions demonstrating that Danilus is indifferent to employee needs. Danilus's management team is considering laying off the workers and implementing a hiring plan, the thinking being that the interviewing and training process will be completed in advance of the plant opening, minimizing downtime once the safety violations are corrected. Some executives, however, favor avoiding layoffs; they want to pay workers while the plant is closed, ensuring that the plant will open and be up and running as soon as possible after the violations are corrected.

The first option has a number of drawbacks from a trust standpoint. Although the layoffs may make financial sense, they don't make sense from a relationship perspective. It essentially punishes all the employees who were already being punished by having to work in an unsafe environment. Given the other labor problems Danilus has experienced, this massive layoff is sure to hurt morale. It would also be unrealistic to assume that many of the laid-off workers will be willing to return; some will find jobs in the interim while others will be so furious with the organization that they won't want to return. Externally, it might lead to negative publicity, hurting recruitment, an especially negative outcome considering that the company hopes to replace laid-off workers.

The second option may create a better relationship with the employees of the closed plant, but at what price? As soon as other employees learn of what Danilus did, they will expect the same overly generous treatment. Danilus will be setting a standard that is impossible to meet consistently, and it's sure to cause friction when the company can't meet high expectations for raises, bonuses, and so on. Just as significantly, the cost of paying workers to do nothing for up to two months will not earn the trust of shareholders; it will come off as the irresponsible act of an organization trying desperately to make amends for previous bad behavior.

Therefore, Danilus should pursue a third option. Danilus knows that about 20 percent of the plant's employees are high performers. It needs to take steps to make sure it doesn't lose these high performers or their trust. This means formulating a plan designed to keep these people from seeking employment elsewhere while the plant is shut down. For instance, Danilus can keep these people on the payroll and assign them to other duties at corporate headquarters during the hiatus. It might also want to offer some of them bonuses and raises as incentives to stay with the company. Although it may lose some of the employees it lays off, that's an acceptable price to pay if it can retain most of its best people. Trust isn't an all-or-nothing proposition. A balance has to be achieved between maintaining employee relationships and being financially responsible. This third option isn't an ideal solution, but it is a balanced one that will help strengthen trust with some key employees.

This shouldn't be where Danilus's efforts end. If Danilus had been the type of company that had been making trust bank deposits all along, it would have a much easier time of maintaining trust during the plant closing. As things stand, though, it needs to start repairing the damage caused by earlier incidents. To rebuild trust internally, Danilus needs to demonstrate to all its employees that it's going to clean up its act. This might mean implementing a plan to improve working conditions at all its plants or raising the pay scale for all high performers. Whatever the action might be, it should send the message that Danilus is going to change in ways that benefit employees.

SCENARIO 2.

Maxto Corporation is a midsize appliance manufacturer. It just brought out a retro-looking toaster that is selling very well, but a quality control employee has noticed that a manufacturing flaw has resulted in slight but noticeable discoloration of the toaster shell. No customers have complained about this flaw, but the toaster is positioned as a premium product and its stylish design is emphasized in advertising and packaging. Maxto executives are struggling with how to deal with this situation, worried that if they recall products and fix the problem, they may be making a mountain out of a molehill and will develop a reputation for poor quality products.

The easiest thing to do is nothing. Because the discoloration is slight and has no impact on product performance, Maxto executives are tempted to fix the problem in the manufacturing process but not take any additional actions. This will limit costs and the possibility of negative feedback from customers and retailers. From a trust standpoint, however, the easiest thing to do is often the *worst* thing.

Certainly Maxto should fix the manufacturing problem. If it doesn't inform customers and retailers about the flaw, however, it's running a significant risk of harming these critical relationships. Cover-ups are never a good idea, even when you're covering up only minor problems. To keep news of this flaw quiet, the company might have to issue internal memos asking employees not to disclose anything about the flaw to suppliers, customers, etc. If this memo ever became "public," it would have an adverse effect on the company's reputation. In fact, the cover-up would be far worse from a trust standpoint than the flaw in the toaster.

The right strategy, therefore, is to contact both customers and retailers about the flaw. Sending letters to customers explaining and apologizing for the problem and giving them the option of exchanging their old toaster for a new, flawless version makes sense. Maxto should also inform retailers about the problem. This open, honest attitude builds trust; it communicates that Maxto is so concerned about product quality that it's willing to be proactive about a minor problem. Certainly Maxto is taking a risk by disclosing the flaw—it could result in negative publicity and people demanding their money back—but that risk is outweighed by the trust reward.

SCENARIO 3.

Jalus Real Estate, a national real estate company, has just completed a record-setting year. Its advertising has long stressed the company's care and concern for both employees and customers; Jalus often is mentioned in surveys as being one of the best companies to work for because of its culture, generous benefits, and competitive salaries. Jalus, though, has come under criticism for a lack of involvement in community programs to feed and house the homeless—programs that many of Jalus's competitors are involved in. An editorial in a national publication takes Jalus to task for spending over $1 million on an employee fitness center yet allocating far less annually to charitable causes.

Perhaps in response to this article, a not-for-profit association contacts Jalus and asks it to help fund a multimillion-dollar project to provide housing for the homeless. Jalus's management is tempted to partici-pate in the project, even though the funding request is huge. Jalus rationalizes that it just had a great year and can afford to make the investment. In addition, it had been looking for ways to become more involved in charitable causes even before the editorial appeared, and the not-for-profit seems to offer a good opportunity to achieve that goal.

Jalus's CFO, however, raises the issue of whether this is the right op-portunity. At a management meeting, he asks, "What are we going to do for an encore?" He notes that the company is in a highly cycli-cal business and next year could be the worst in its history. He won-ders if it would be wise to make this huge investment and create expectations that this is the type of thing Jalus is going to do every year. Plus, the not-for-profit told Jalus that the project is ongoing, and it hopes Jalus will continue to support it year after year. Jalus worries about what will happen if it has to reduce the investment by 50 per-cent the following year and if such an event might undo the goodwill it has built.

Jalus's CFO is correct. Organizations that make huge commit-ments to charitable projects without much planning often end up regretting it. Just because a good cause presents itself doesn't mean it's the *right* cause for the company. Not only does it need to do its homework—finding out more about the not-for-profit and analyzing whether it's a good fit for Jalus—but it should also think about starting its external trust-building efforts on a smaller scale. Jalus doesn't want to create the impression that it is making the donation in response to the editorial—an impression such a huge donation might create.

When companies haven't been active in pro bono causes, community activities, and charitable giving, they need to test the waters to find out what's right for them. This means appointing a team to investigate all the opportunities available and not just the one that comes knocking. It may turn out that Jalus decides to donate a smaller sum of money to the not-for-profit that approached it as well as become involved in supporting two or three other causes on a smaller scale. After an initial test period, Jalus can then determine where it is best able to use its resources for a good cause and where the biggest trust payback will come from.

SCENARIO 4.

A young, rapidly growing software company, Omnibyte, has been too busy building its business to give much thought to trust-building activities. Just hiring enough people to keep up with the expanding workload is a challenge. During the past year, however, a number of Omnibyte employees have been lobbying management to become involved in a "save-the-earth" group started by a famous rock-and-roll musician. The employees have argued that too many software companies staffed by young people are viewed as overly self-involved and not particularly concerned about social and environmental issues; they feel that by participating in this group they will help Omnibyte avoid being categorized in this way.

Omnibyte's CEO, Joan, agrees with her employees' assessment up to a point. An environmentalist and feminist herself, Joan has always

had the impulse to devote a portion of Omnibyte's resources to so-
cially responsible causes. She wonders, though, if this is the right
cause. Although she admires the goals of the save-the-earth group,
she also has reservations about the rock musician who heads it. This
musician has had a number of brushes with the law, including arrests
for drug use and contributing to the delinquency of a minor. Though
the musician claims to have changed, there have been rumors that
he's still using drugs and generally leading an unsavory lifestyle.

Joan doesn't want to alienate employees advocating involvement
with this group. They are some of her best and brightest people, and
she recognizes that they feel strongly about this issue (though she
suspects they feel strongly, in part, because they are fans of this musician's music). Joan has a meeting scheduled with these employees to
make a decision on this matter, and she's not sure how to orchestrate
the discussion so that the right decision is reached.

It's not unusual for companies to face situations where internal trust is weighed against external trust. Sometimes organizations make large donations to charitable groups and employees
grumble that the money should have been used for employee bonuses and salaries. In other instances, organizations are so concerned about repairing low morale or poor management-
employee relationships that they don't spend the necessary time
or money building external relationships.

Joan shouldn't make the mistake of choosing one over the
other. She shouldn't simply dismiss her employees' wishes or give
in to them. One danger at their upcoming meeting, though, is
that Joan will be swayed by their passionate commitment to a
good cause and give in to their request. Another danger is that
she will alienate them by curtly telling them that they're naive
and starstruck.

In these situations, the right course of action is to empower the internal people to come up with a viable external strategy. During their meeting, Joan should explain that she's hesitant to involve Omnibyte with the save-the-earth group because of the musician's unsavory reputation. Rather than vetoing the idea out of hand, Joan should ask the group of employees to come up with alternative worthy causes. Though Joan should communicate that she hopes they'll come up with other ideas that better suit Omnibyte's values, she shouldn't close the door completely on the save-the-earth group. The odds are that her employees will close the door for her by finding a more deserving organization.

SCENARIO 5.

William has just been appointed CEO of one of the country's largest corporations, and at his first executive staff meeting, he talks eloquently and passionately about the need for the company to "give back" to the community. He explains that he and his wife have been very active in raising funds for research involving a rare childhood blood disease; William talks about how they lost their son to this disease when he was only three and they've been involved in fundraising since then. Everyone in the staff meeting defers to William; the force of his emotional argument is so powerful that they feel like they would be insensitive if they were to object.

When William tells the company's public relations firm of his plan, however, it points out that there may be other possibilities it should consider. The head of the public relations firm's account team explains that though he's sure research for this blood disorder is necessary and important work, it's not the cause he would recommend the company adopt as its own. He says that because the company is one of the largest in the world, it should find a cause suitable to its size. There are only five hundred children in the United States afflicted by the blood disorder, and this public relations executive argues that the company could use its resources to help find a cure for a disease that impacts millions of kids.

William is confused about the right course of action. He knows that research for rare diseases is traditionally underfunded, and he believes that his company can do more good by giving money to an underfunded cause than one that is "popular." He makes the point to the public relations executive that if the company's involvement results in a cure for this rare blood disease, it will receive far more favorable recognition by all its stakeholders than if it contributes to a more popular cause. William realizes that part of his motivation is his wife's involvement with the blood disorder foundation—she serves on its board—but he also feels that the company shouldn't jump on a popular, charitable bandwagon where it would just be one of many corporate contributors.

CEOs frequently involve their organizations in *personal* causes and crusades. They have the best of intentions but don't always get the best of results. Personal and corporate agendas don't necessarily mesh. In this instance, William's emotional involvement is affecting his judgment. His organization should find a cause suited to its size and, more important, that fits its strategic objectives. Although William's point is well taken—that if it helps find a cure for the blood disorder, the company will be hailed for its contributions—there's no guarantee that a cure will be found. More significantly, it's likely that William is overestimating the response even if a cure is found. Although the company may be "hailed," it won't be hailed for long or loudly. Rightly or wrongly, people (including the media) pay more attention to breakthroughs involving "name" diseases.

William suggests that the company should avoid these name diseases and focus on ones where research efforts are underfunded. His inference is that the company shouldn't take a me-too approach, and this is a valid point. But the best way for the company to distinguish itself is by crafting a unique strategy for helping others. Focusing on only the particular charity or group to which it will donate funds is shortsighted. The larger issue is what form this involvement will take. Does it make particularly good use of a company's resources? Does it communicate the company's deep commitment to a particular cause? Does the charitable effort dovetail with the company's products and services, culture, and size? And finally, does it make your employees feel proud? These are the questions that should be answered before deciding on a course of action.

SCENARIO 6.

ElectroSell is a manufacturer of consumer electronics, and it has introduced a camcorder that is selling extremely well. ElectroSell executives, however, have just received a report from R&D informing them that new technology is likely to make this camcorder obsolete in two years, that a new generation of products will provide superior quality and features.

ElectroSell is a highly ethical company. It has always taken pride in living its values, and some executives believe that they should create a plan to phase out the product. In a staff meeting, one executive advocates informing camcorder customers about this new technology and offering them rebates when the new product comes out. He says, "If we don't do this, our customers will resent us for selling them products we knew were going to be obsolete in the near future."

The CEO, however, is concerned that such a rebate program would cost the company millions of dollars. He also isn't sure if its customers would be resentful if a new generation of products emerges. At the same time, he believes that ElectroSell has a higher ethical standard to uphold than most companies, and he wants to be sure that it maintains the strong customer relationships it has enjoyed for many years.

ElectroSell is overreacting to this problem. Although it's admirable that executives are highly conscious of ethical issues, they also need to put these issues in perspective. This can be difficult, in that in other areas of life—politics, medicine, etc.—full disclosure might be warranted. You want your doctor to tell you if a new drug that will soon receive FDA approval is a better choice than your current medication.

In this consumer electronics area, however, customers are accustomed to rapid technological changes. They know that DVDs are replacing VCRs and that compact discs have replaced records. It is unreasonable to expect that a company would sabotage a product that's selling well just because a new technology *might* make it obsolete in two years. Most customers wouldn't expect a rebate, especially if a company creates a superior product. Unlike our previous example of the flawed toaster, there's nothing wrong with ElectroSell's product. To make this rebate offer to customers would also anger retailers, which would probably lose a significant amount of revenue until the new product came out.

When the new camcorder is produced and ready to ship, ElectroSell might then offer a discount to its customer base or provide some other type of customer loyalty reward. Treating customers fairly is crucial, but the fairness standard is determined by *reasonable* customer expectations.

SCENARIO 7.

Campton Inc. is a national chain of home improvement stores, and over the years it has done a good job of building its trust bank. Campton has been involved in community activities, contributed money to charities, and established open, honest relationships with customers and the media. Aside from a few labor problems—there was a threat of a strike a few years ago—Campton has rarely received negative publicity. Then a former employee entered one of its stores, took out a gun, and began shooting. After he had killed three customers and wounded eight others, he killed himself.

Campton executives aren't sure how to handle this tragedy. They feel there was nothing they could have done to prevent this maniac from entering their store and shooting people. Though he was a former employee, he hadn't been fired, and his boss said he had left on good terms. In addition, the Campton store where he had worked was in another state. Though his motivation for the rampage was unclear, the man had left a rambling, semi-incoherent note that referred to Campton as an "evil corporation."

There's a great deal of disagreement about how to deal with this event among the team Campton has assembled. Some editorials right after the shooting blamed Campton for not having better security— the security guard in this store, like all Campton security people, wasn't armed, and he did exactly what he was told to do in this type of event: call the police. Members of Campton's team noted that some employees have been making sick jokes about how working for Campton could drive anyone crazy. They worry that some employees as well as some outside observers may speculate that working conditions at Campton aren't all they should be. There are other Campton executives, however, who are resisting taking any specific actions in response to the shooting. They say that if they institute new security procedures or do anything for the families of victims, it would be akin to an admission of guilt. Fearing lawsuits from the victims' families and attacks by the media, they want Campton to issue a statement saying that though the company sympathizes with the families, it was powerless to prevent this tragedy.

Many times the best trust strategies in the wake of crises occupy the middle ground. If Campton were to issue a statement that was defensive or refused to accept blame, it would appear to be heartless, even though that wasn't its intent. Remember my story of the billboard of a gravestone and the headline: "He had the right of way"? Just because you're right doesn't mean you

should cloak yourself in moral purity. Perception is more important than reality: The public associates a mad killer with the
Campton store name. As a result, it seems responsible in some
way for the violence that occurred in the store and was committed by a former employee.

At the same time, Campton should not overreact to the shooting and act as if it really was responsible. It shouldn't talk about
how it needs to have better security procedures or how it should
have identified the killer's emotional problems when he was an
employee. Not only would this overreaction make Campton appear more responsible than it really was, but it could hurt the
company if lawsuits are filed.

The middle-ground strategy Campton should pursue involves
finding a way to do good. Campton executives should react "naturally"; they should be shocked and saddened by what happened
and resolve to do what they can to heal the emotional wounds
caused by the shooting. It would be appropriate for them to become involved in a victims' rights group or provide employees
with greater access to therapeutic services. They might want to
contribute to handgun control campaigns or to create an education fund for children of the people who were killed by the gun-
man. Expressing sympathy and following it up with sympathetic
actions is the best way to rebuild trust that might have been lost.
Campton, because it had established a trust bank, is in a good
position to regain trust if it does the right thing.

SCENARIO 8.

For the past five years, Gentell Financial Services has had one record
year after the next. Its salespeople have a reputation for being highly
aggressive—some of Gentell's critics call them too aggressive—and
they have made a major contribution to Gentell's growth. More so
than others in their industry, Gentell's salespeople use high-pressure
selling tactics on customers and do everything possible to maximize

income from the account. Working on a commission system, these salespeople have ample incentive to maximize income. A few salespeople have been accused of churning customer accounts, but Gentell's internal investigation revealed no wrongdoing.

Gentell has recently received a slew of customer complaints about its practices; people claim some salespeople have made promises they didn't keep about investments, exaggerating the return investors could expect or assuring them about the safety of certain investment vehicles. Gentell has always had its share of these types of complaints—they are received by every company in the industry—but the number has increased dramatically. Just as troubling, an investigative team from a local newspaper has posed as customers and recorded the telephone pitches of Gentell salespeople, and the transcripts clearly indicate that some Gentell people have crossed the line.

Gentell's CEO is alarmed by these practices and wants to stop them, but he is worried that the result may be a more ethical but less profitable company.

Understandably, the CEO doesn't want to do anything to reduce profits. What he should understand, though, is that a less ethical company will be a less profitable one in the long run. Even though Gentell has been highly successful over a five-year period, it will have to pay for this success if it has been achieved through questionable means. Customer complaints and negative publicity are only the first two shots across its bow. Eventually, government regulatory bodies will become involved and customers will depart. No one likes doing business with a *morally* bankrupt company.

Many companies face decisions about how to handle a highly productive but "difficult" employee. Difficult can mean anything from problems getting along with other people to acting in irresponsible or unethical ways. When you feel embarrassed that

someone is representing your company, that's usually a clear in-
dication that you need to get rid of him. These bad apples don't
cause problems with just external stakeholders but impact internal people as well. At Gentell, employees saw that unethical but
productive behavior was rewarded, and they naturally adopted
this behavior.

To restore trust, Gentell needs to fire the worst offenders and
set up a system with teeth to discourage others from pursuing
questionable practices. This may mean bringing in coaches to
work with people whose borderline behaviors require that they
change or leave. It may involve setting up a clearly defined three-
strikes-and-you're-out system so that negative sanctions discourage unethical actions. It may require more stringent monitoring
of salespeople. And the CEO must make it clear to everyone that
it's no longer business as usual. Only when people realize that
he's serious about changing how the company operates will they
make an effort to change.

SCENARIO 9.

Mangrove Corporation has been in the news a great deal lately, and
the news hasn't been good. The board has accepted the CEO's and
CFO's resignations in the wake of a stock manipulation scandal, and
a number of other executives involved in the scandal have been fired.
Mangrove has been taken to task in the media and by government
regulators for its blatant disregard of its stockholders and employees—both lost a lot of money because of the machinations—and
Mangrove had been characterized by one regulator as being beset
by "a culture of greed."

Mangrove has brought in a new CEO with a sterling reputation to
nurse the corporation back to health. It has a good core business, but
sales have dropped significantly because of all the negative publicity.
Long-standing relationships with customers have ended, the financial

community views the company with a jaundiced eye, and morale is terrible.

The new CEO wants to make a big splash, to do something significant to signify that Mangrove has changed. In meetings with the board, he has suggested that Mangrove do things like setting aside 5 percent of its profits annually for good causes or funding a foundation dedicated to fostering strong business ethics. Other board members wonder if this is a wise use of money at a time when Mangrove is not in the best financial position. One board member suggests that Mangrove do nothing in terms of restoring trust until everything blows over, explaining that anything that it does at this point is likely to be questioned or viewed with suspicion.

Neither the new CEO nor the board has hit upon the right strategy. Certainly it would be a mistake for Mangrove to make a big show of doing good. Such a gesture probably would be misinterpreted, viewed as a big company trying to buy back trust. In addition, one big move such as this won't heal the broken bonds with all stakeholders. Mangrove has alienated customers, the financial community, shareholders, employees, and the general public. It needs to focus trust-building strategies on each group.

Keeping a low profile for a while is a good idea, but it's a *bad* idea to do *nothing.* Although the passing of time will allow Mangrove to slip out of the spotlight, it won't erase the bad feelings it's created. People who have been hurt by Mangrove will hold on to their negative feelings about the company for a long time unless Mangrove is proactive about repairing the damage.

The appropriate course of action would be to launch a series of small-scale projects targeting each group where relationships have been damaged. It can be as simple as a series of town hall meetings with employees to clear the air. It might involve editorial board meetings to communicate the CEO's vision for Mangrove. A plan should be created for *starting* to build trust, limited to no more than the next six months. It should consist of a number of viable projects, all of which are designed to communicate that Mangrove is sincere about doing everything it can to restore relationships.

10

The Media: How to Develop Relationships That Build Trust

The pure and simple truth is rarely pure and never simple.

—OSCAR WILDE

Many corporate leaders approach the media in ways that ultimately build distrust rather than trust. They accuse reporters of slanting stories to make their companies seem greedy and coldhearted. They provide the media with little of substance, attempting to charm their way into favorable coverage. They refuse to talk to representatives of certain publications and shows because they are convinced that they're out to get them. They attempt to manipulate and bully the media in order to get the stories they want. They talk down to reporters, believing they have relatively little business acumen.

The media can be an ally in helping organizations restore and maintain trust, but not if they're treated with arrogance, condescension, or indifference. The media aren't perfect. Some reporters can be biased and some publications and programs thrive on sensationalistic journalism. They can misinterpret information and get the facts wrong, resulting in a story that causes a company harm. And there are media representatives who are vulnerable to a leader's charisma.

None of this, however, should dictate a company's media strategy. In general, the media are like everyone else: If you treat them fairly, they'll treat you fairly. Similarly, if you don't trust them, they won't trust you.

To a certain extent, you can't control what the media report. If a company does something wrong and it's sufficiently newsworthy, the media will nail it. What a company can control are certain aspects of the process. By communicating clearly and consistently with the media, management can make sure a reporter conveys the tremendous commitment of the company's employees to a particular charitable endeavor. It may be able to establish a solid relationship with a reporter covering the industry, receiving the benefit of the doubt when a crisis hits. The cumulative impact of these and other actions is significant. Some companies are terrific at media relations, and the trust they've built with stakeholders is due in no small part to how the media cover them.

To achieve this media relations goal, the first step is ridding yourself of the misconceptions that hamper trust-building efforts.

Myths, Misconceptions, and Other Damaging Media Beliefs

Some misconceptions about how to deal with the media have a historical basis. Years ago, reporters were more likely to play favorites, and some of them could be bribed with gifts. Years ago, media people were often not as sophisticated about business as they are today and it was easier to manipulate them.

Other misconceptions are rooted in a single, negative experience. If an executive is burned by a reporter who makes public his off-the-record comments, he reflexively labels all reporters as duplicitous.

Whatever the reason for the misconceptions, it's important to rid yourself of them. To that end, here are some of the most common ones.

The Best Media Approach Is to Duck Them When You Have Bad News and Court Them When You Have Good News

Ducking the media when the company is experiencing problems is a common tactic. Who wants to be cross-examined about these problems and how you may have caused them? Though talking about bad news isn't any fun, it's often what you need to do if you want to establish good relationships with reporters. When you refuse to take their calls, it communicates that you have something to hide or that you're embarrassed about something your company has done. Reporters arc trained to have a certain amount of healthy skepticism, and ducking turns that skepticism into suspicion. I know some top executives who hardly ever speak to reporters on negative subjects, even after their public relations people clear the decks for them.

These same executives, however, are very forthcoming when things are going well. They are generous with their time and information, perhaps believing that this generosity will compensate for their previous stonewalling. It won't. Reporters appreciate consistency. The alternating pattern of ducking and openness makes them furious. It sends the message that "I'll talk to you *only* when I *want* to talk to you." This arrogance is not the way to create a mutually beneficial relationship with the media.

The Media Can Be Manipulated

I've known CEOs and other senior executives who assume that most reporters really don't understand core business issues. As a result, they feel they can talk about strategy or financial matters without fear that the reporter will see the flaws in their logic. What they don't realize is that even if reporters don't have MBAs or have never worked in a corporation, many of them have covered the business world long enough that they are highly attuned to the way it operates. And they take great delight in surprising manipulative executives with their knowledge.

I witnessed such an encounter when a reporter from a business publication was interviewing a Fortune 500 CEO. He was explaining an accounting issue to her and interrupted his explanation, saying, "*You* probably wouldn't understand this." He was a macho guy who looked down not only on reporters but also on women; he was making the assumption that because she was a woman and a reporter, she couldn't possibly grasp the subtle accounting matter. Not only did she get it—she let this CEO have it then and there—but her story reflected her anger at him and portrayed him in a negative light.

I've also had clients who, when it was clear that a negative story was being written, asked me to intervene, saying something like, "Use your public relations razzle dazzle." (They must have really been impressed by the musical *Chicago*.) It was as if they believed the media were vulnerable to some sort of public relations magic, that I could call a reporter and say something—I'm not quite sure what—and dissuade him from pursuing the story. Most print and broadcast reporters are highly professional and take great pride in their work, and to attempt to get them to be less than professional is asking for trouble.

Finally, some businesspeople believe they can use their charm to manipulate reporters. This is especially true of highly charismatic leaders who are skilled at getting others to do what they want. President Clinton, for one, was accustomed to charming everyone he met, and for a while, it worked. The problem is that this charm is only short-lived and effective in certain circumstances. In Clinton's case, once the charm wore off and circumstances changed, reporters went after him with their teeth bared. Similarly, business leaders find that their charm has only a temporary effect. Former CEOs like GE's Jack Welch, Sears' Arthur Martinez, and Microsoft's Bill Gates seemed protected by their charisma, but eventually the media ignored it and started asking hard questions and writing negative stories.

If You Cut Off Communication, You Deprive Reporters of the Information Necessary to Write a Story

I've saved the biggest myth for last. When reporters start digging about a story that could have negative trust consequences for a company, the company sometimes cuts off communication with the media on the assumption that sharks don't feed unless there's blood in the water. The reasoning goes that if reporters can't interview anyone in the company or obtain information that corroborates their story's assumptions, they won't do the story.

Although this may be true is some instances, more often than not, the reporter will write the story anyway, and the company won't have the opportunity to put forth its point of view. I'm not advocating telling the media *everything* in *every* situation—some facts can be easily misinterpreted by both the media and the public—but it's important to provide at least some information so reporters can do their jobs. An aggressive news person who digs hard enough and long enough will gather sufficient data to do the story sooner or later, with or without a given company's cooperation.

Understand Who You're Dealing With: What Drives the Media

To increase the odds that the media help rather than hinder your trust-building efforts, you must have realistic expectations of the media. Although every reporter is a different person with different goals—and though there are differences between print and broadcast, national and local publications, and so on—journalists are generally looking for the big story. Exposés fall in this category, as do corporate crises. They love to be first with the big story, and though they may feel sorry for the CEO with his hand caught in the cookie jar or the company whose oil tanker springs a leak, they're not going to go easy on either of them no matter how they feel.

Therefore, don't harbor unrealistic expectations for your media relations efforts. No reporter worth his salt is going to give you or your company a pass just because you've built a strong relationship with him. What reporters might do, however, is give you the benefit of the doubt. If you tell them that you'd like them to wait a day or two before they do a story because you're gathering information that you believe will impact the story, they may agree to wait. They may also give your quotes a little more prominence or call some of the sources you provide or use the angle you suggest to them. Cumulatively, all this can make a difference.

Second, recognize that reporters really are interested in "man bites dog" stories and are disinterested in the dog bites man types. I've seen too many business executives convinced they were offering reporters a great opportunity to do a wonderful story, when in reality they were simply offering them a chance to do a puff piece. Just because you're donating $1 million to a charity doesn't mean it's a big story to the reporter and her readers; it may simply be a big story only for your company. You may have launched what you feel is a highly innovative benefits program, but the reporter may know of ten other programs that are similar to it.

This is why you can't just do good deeds and expect it to be automatically heralded by the media. You need to be creative in how you do good things and perhaps even take risks and be provocative in what you do. Too often, companies try to create trust in conservative, ordinary ways when they should be bold and precedent setting. It's the latter approach that appeals to reporters.

How to Translate Trust-Building Deeds into Media Language

Admittedly, the media are unreliable partners in your trust-building efforts. They have their own agenda, and helping your company achieve a good relationship with all its stakeholders isn't on it. Nonetheless, you can take certain actions that will increase the odds that the media will communicate the messages you want to get across to various audiences. Here are some steps that all organizations can take.

Apply the Trust Bank Concept to Your Media Relationships

A major corporation has been slapped with an employee discrimination lawsuit by five former employees who are minorities. The CEO has ample evidence the lawsuit is frivolous, and there's no question that it will quickly be dismissed by a judge. In the interim, though, the lawsuit could cause big problems for the company, which is currently in the midst of a major hiring push—many of the people who work in the company's plants are minorities. The CEO hopes to convince the media that the lawsuit is frivolous and that the company has a long record of hiring minorities and excellent labor relations. Unfortunately, the company doesn't have a record of good media relations. It's not that it has treated reporters poorly, but that it has mostly taken media relationships for granted. Management never made much of an effort to nurture these relationships, and at times reacted with indifference to reporters' requests for information. As a result, there isn't much equity built up in the company's media relationships, and its request for a little leeway is likely to fall on deaf ears.

Too often, companies view media relationships as short term. They devote much effort to a major press release or news conference announcing a great new product and relatively little effort to building and sustaining media relationships. Creating a trust bank with the media means communicating regularly with key reporters (such as the ones who cover your industry for significant business publications). This doesn't just mean taking them out to lunch and schmoozing with them. It requires a continuous exchange of ideas and information. You want journalists to understand what makes your company tick. If you're doing all these wonderful things for employees, customers, and the community, show reporters what they are. They may not write a single word about these activities, but they'll develop an appreciation for the company's beliefs and values. When they do decide to do a story about the company, their understanding of these beliefs and values will influence their tone. Just as significantly, when the company runs into problems, the media will be more likely to treat the company fairly.

One other media trust bank tactic: Discover what a reporter's requirements and interests are rather than just communicating those of the company. Many organizations are so intent on getting their various points across that they create unequal relationships. They never learn what business issues are of particular interest to a reporter; they never take the time to understand what her publication's or program's needs are and how she's trying to meet them. Making this effort not only helps a company learn what types of information will snare a reporter's interest, but it's a sign of good faith, a way of demonstrating that you consider the reporter's requirements important.

Make an Effort to Tell Your Side of the Story

This may seem obvious in theory, but it's often ignored in practice. When a publication or program is working on a story that a company knows (or suspects) will be negative, the company frequently refuses to speak to a reporter. This is almost always a mistake. Though you can't turn a negative piece into a positive one, your goal should be to "own" a quote in the story or a paragraph that states your company's viewpoint. That quote may help you reassure a customer or calm employee fears. It may not seem like much within the scope of the article, but it may be enough to maintain the bond of trust with certain readers, viewers, or listeners.

Although companies generally don't have formal policies about speaking to the media, informal ones often prevent people from getting their side of the story into print. We had a client who was furious that its main competitor was receiving more favorable coverage than it was, including credit for innovations that our client was responsible for. It turned out that the brand managers at this company had discovered the fastest way to get in trouble with their bosses was to be quoted in business publications. For this reason, they clammed up when reporters called. It was only when the CEO of this company became aware of the problem and helped catalyze a culture shift that these brand managers became comfortable talking to reporters, and once they did, the organization received more favorable coverage.

At the same time, don't be *naive*. Some reporters are dead set on slamming certain companies. Others have no choice, given the negative events that have led up to the story. In these instances, it's generally better to have one good paragraph than none at all. A number of years ago, syndicated columnist Jack Anderson wanted to interview one of our clients who had contributed money to a political campaign and had allegedly received favors from this elected official in return. Knowing this client as I did, I was absolutely certain these charges were false, and I advised him to talk to Anderson. I qualified my advice by saying that talking to him didn't mean Anderson would change his point of view.

Our client talked with Anderson, who not only didn't change his point of view but wrote a hatchet piece. Still, the client didn't blame me or believe he made the wrong choice by talking to Anderson. The saving grace was a quote from our client, a small but significant refutation of the charges. It wasn't much, but it was enough to demonstrate that everything wasn't as cut and dried as Anderson made it seem.

Use a Multilevel, Multidimensional Approach

Creating trust is a complex and at times subtle process. One positive story isn't going to do it. It often requires a variety of media exposures over a sustained period of time before attitudes change. Don't set your sights exclusively on a *Fortune* magazine cover story or a major *Wall Street Journal* piece. Those are great, but they're also short-lived. Trust begins to grow when your targeted audience reads a story on your company in a trade journal, hears your CEO (or other executive) speaking at a trade conference, notices your company on a ten-best list, reads an op-ed piece written by someone in your company, browses through a company newsletter, and reads a Web site feature on your company. The cumulative impact of all these exposures to your trust-building activities is what will cause people to increase their trust in your organization.

You must hit a number of different notes. One article may matter-of-factly explain how your company is helping to feed starving children in Africa. An executive from your company, on the other hand, may give a keynote address at a major industry conference where he speaks with great passion and eloquence about your effort to help starving children. A third exposure might be a PBS documentary that shows how volunteers from your company as well as other organizations use their business acumen to make sure food reaches the right people at the right time.

There is an art as much as a science to working with media to create trust. The multidimensional approach for a company that is trying to recover from a financial scandal is different from that for an organization that is attempting to increase the level of trust customers place in the company. To some extent, the process involves trial-and-error. One message may work with print publications but not interest broadcast media. You may discover that the Internet is the best way to reach and impact a particular stakeholder group. There are many different media approaches, and you shouldn't limit yourself to just one.

Be Prepared: Why the Boy Scout Motto Comes in Handy

A company can do all the right things with regard to the media, but if its key spokesperson (or spokespeople) isn't effective, then the company's trust message may be lost. Some leaders I've mentioned, such as Ray Kroc, Jack Welch, and Lee Iacocca, were terrific when dealing with journalists. Whether instinctively or through training, they enjoyed great credibility with all types of reporters. These CEOs, though, took this responsibility seriously. Ralph Larsen, the former CEO of Johnson & Johnson and another great media person, told me he devoted approximately 75 percent of his time to communication externally and internally.

Not all CEOs assign communication responsibilities such a high priority. Many view media chores as a burden, believing they should be spending their time running the company rather than talking about it. In other instances, they're willing to take on these responsibilities but aren't particularly good at them; they appear to be indecisive, inconsistent, or inarticulate when talking to media representatives.

Whether you're a CEO or anyone else who has regular media interactions, you need to prepare yourself for this function. The most basic aspect of preparation is acquainting yourself with the variety of ways your company is building trust. If you're not directly involved with some of these endeavors, you need to take the time to talk to the right people and read the relevant materials. Reporters respect knowledge, and if you come off as unknowledgeable about all the great things you're doing for shareholders, employees, and the community, reporters won't consider them great.

Beyond this basic task, a spokesperson has to be prepared for common (and sometimes, uncommon) situations. For instance, one situation that might come up is a reporter from a major publication requesting an interview, and as much as you want to grant this request, you can't for legal reasons or because you'll jeopardize a deal that's in the works. If you find yourself in this situation, would you:

A. Say, "No comment" and provide no further explanation.

B. Instruct your people to tell the reporter that you've been called away on a business emergency and won't be available for at least one week.

C. Promise the reporter the biggest story of his life if he lets you slide this time.

D. None of the above.

D is the correct answer. Turning down a request from a major publication is a big deal. There are circumstances when it has to be done, but if you want to maintain a good relationship with this reporter, you need to give him something besides a "no comment" or a lie. To create or maintain a trusting relationship, you might suggest another source for the story the reporter is pursuing or explain precisely why you have to decline his request. Here are three trust-building ways to decline an interview:

- I can't talk about the specific accident because it's the subject of litigation, but I'd be happy to discuss our overall safety record and how it leads the industry.

- I'm not an expert on the head tax, but I can give you the name of a woman with our industry's trade association who can provide you with the details. Also, the amount of tax our company pays is a matter of record, and I can share that information with you.

- We don't discuss specific personnel matters out of respect for the individual's privacy. Our company's policy on this issue goes as follows . . .

Slickly avoiding questions, telling lies, or launching minifilibusters will alienate reporters sooner or later. In some circumstances, you need to be prepared to offer the media fair disclosure rather than full disclosure. This may not make reporters happy, but it will help maintain their respect. Secretary of Defense Donald Rumsfeld is respected by most reporters who cover him, even though he frequently refuses to give them the detailed answers they'd like to have. When he doesn't want to answer a question, he says so, but he follows up that refusal with the reason for it. Rumsfeld is usually very well prepared for his media interactions, though he's been known to let his guard down and alienate a few of our foreign leaders at times.

Preparation can take many forms, but from a trust standpoint, the following are the most important.

Create a Succinct, Powerful Message to Communicate in Media Interviews

For many executives, boiling down their trust messages is tough. A large corporation may be involved in all sorts of charitable projects, employee benefits innovations, and customer programs that demonstrate the corporation's commitment and caring. It's impossible to capture all of this in one story. Nonetheless, executives try to jam everything into the interview, leaving the reporter and ultimately his audience confused about what exactly the company is doing.

We once had a client who declined our offer of media training, explaining he knew what he wanted to say and showed us a twenty-two-page copy of a speech he recently delivered. Our offer was the result of an upcoming television interview in which he'd be on the air for no more than three minutes. We knew that if this business leader, as articulate as he was, did the interview by relying on his twenty-two pages, it would be a mess. There was just no way he would be able to communicate key points; he'd come off as rambling and unfocused. For this reason, the person heading this account responded to the executive's "I know what I want to say" by telling him, "What you *want* to say doesn't count. What's important is what you *need* to say and how to say it in the time allowed."

Before interviews, rehearse how you're going to communicate your message. Specifically, think about the trust issue involved and how you're going to explain it (a looming strike, a product safety issue, etc.); focus on what your company is doing to address this issue; specify the benefits to the audience involved. It should take only a few sentences to communicate this "essence." Obviously, you may have more time to elaborate on these points. But the key is to make sure this message is crystal clear. Interviews are highly subjective experiences, and a reporter can easily miss what you think is the most important point unless you're prepared to communicate it with clarity.

Be Ready for the Tough Questions

No matter how good you are at thinking on your feet or how well-versed you are in the subject that the interview will revolve around, you need to prepare yourself for questions that don't have easy answers. This is especially true when your company has been involved in a scandal, is in the midst of a crisis, or is facing major financial problems. The odds are that your answers to these questions will be the centerpiece of a reporter's story, and your comments are more likely to create distrust if they're ad-libbed. For instance, a reporter for a major business publication was interviewing a tough-talking CEO about his company's labor problems, and the reporter noted that the company's factory employees were among the lowest paid in the industry and wondered if he thought this was fair. The CEO replied, "Fairness doesn't matter. I have a responsibility to our shareholders that supercedes what's fair." Though the CEO went on to explain how the company was bending over backwards to be fair in the labor negotiations, the quote that received prominence in the article and that was sarcastically featured on strikers' placards was: "Fairness doesn't matter."

Make a list of the toughest questions you can imagine being asked and formulate short and true replies to them. Long-winded generalizations won't work; the reporter will spot them for the hot air they most assuredly are and ignore them.

Some reporters, however, will persist in focusing on the negative. They'll try and trip you up and get you to say something provocative (and potentially distrustful). Keeping your cool is important, but even more important is using "transition tactics" to return to your main message. These tactics can be simple phrases such as, "But the bottom line is . . ." or "Yes, and in addition to that . . ." or "The key thing to remember is . . ." Or you can create your own links to the message you've formulated and rehearsed, steering a response in the direction of this message. Though this may not deter a reporter who is focused on negative issues, it may help put these issues in the context of the message you want to deliver.

Maintain a Balance Between What the Media Need and What the Company Is Willing to Give

In other words, you must prepare a middle-ground response that will satisfy your trust-building goals and the media's need to know. This takes a certain amount of reflection and homework. If you disclose everything to the media, you may make them happy, but the resulting story will hurt your relationship with a stakeholder group. If you disclose only what suits your purposes, you may say the right things to build trust, but the media won't print them because it's not what they're looking for.

In the wake of a record bad quarter, for instance, reporters may be pounding on your door demanding quotes about why revenues fell so precipitously, while you're interested in talking about prospects for future growth. Finding the middle ground between the two will be the key to achieving your goals. You may have to make a bargain with yourself, such as "I'll talk about how we misjudged the pan-Asian market if the reporters allows me to explain our new European strategy." This won't result in the ideal interview, but it will probably help you get certain key points into the story that might otherwise be ignored.

As an old sage once said when describing a newspaper reporter during an interview: "Never argue with someone who buys ink by the barrel!"

CHAPTER 11

Great Acts of Trust

Morals are an acquirement—like music, like a foreign language, like piety, poker, paralysis—no man is born with them.

—MARK TWAIN

rust can be built and restored in countless ways. Although I've suggested certain strategies and tactics that you can use, don't feel limited by these suggestions. In fact, creativity is often necessary to come up with effective trust solutions. The standard operating procedure that might work for five companies may not work for the sixth. Numerous factors impact a company's approach, its past trust bank efforts (or lack thereof), the seriousness of the problems it is addressing, the specifics of a particular event or incident, and so on.

As terrific as Tylenol's response to the tampering crisis was, it may not be the best response for your company, even if you're facing a similar type of product tampering situation. That's why you need to draw upon your people's creativity—and especially the creativity of leaders—to arrive at effective trust-building responses.

To help you in this regard, I'd like to share with you eight great trust strategies. Some are designed to create internal trust, others target external groups. Some of the companies involved are small or midsize, others are large. Some involve inspired CEO leadership in the face of a potential loss of trust, others show different elements of an organization pulling together to maintain its reputation. Although I've included examples throughout the book, the ones used here focus on specific "acts" of trust building. They will give you a sense of what's possible when companies approach trust building with an innovative, committed mindset.

Act #1: Taking Personal Responsibility

What do you do when people die as a result of using a product your company manufactured? Complicating matters, the deaths aren't clearly the fault of your company or the product. Is accepting full responsibility the best way to maintain trust, or is it a "coerced" (by public pressure) guilty plea that will also result in costly lawsuits? Is denying any responsibility the best course of action, or does it open the company to tremendous trust erosion if evidence comes out indicting the company?

In late summer of 2001, fifty-three dialysis patients who were using a Baxter International dialysis filter died in the United States and six other countries. Though people on dialysis often die, the fact that all these patients were using the same filter manufactured from the same place at the same time suggested that the filter was the cause. Then, as now, it remains unclear exactly how the filter caused their deaths. Just as significantly, it was difficult to assign blame to Baxter. In fact, Baxter had just bought the company that manufactured the filters, Althin Medical AB, the previous year.

Baxter immediately recalled all the filters. It also launched in-house and independent investigations that ultimately didn't answer all the questions about the deaths but yielded a hypothesis about the cause. Ultimately, Baxter accepted full responsibility for what took place, even though the investigations didn't reveal that it was guilty of quality control problems or could have prevented the tragedy.

CEO Harry Kraemer, however, decided that despite all the questions surrounding what happened, the bottom line was that a Baxter product was involved and it was impossible to absolve the company of all culpability. From Kraemer's perspective, Baxter was responsible because there was no way of proving beyond the shadow of a doubt that it wasn't responsible.

For this reason, Kraemer issued a public apology. Second, he immediately began a thorough investigation of the problem. Third, he not only recalled the filters in question but shut down Althin, the Baxter company that made the filters, taking a charge to earnings of $189 million. Fourth, Baxter provided financial settlements to the victims' families. Fifth, the company bent over backwards to keep all relevant parties the victims' families, health-care facilities, competitors that may have been using the same filter manufacturing process—informed about developments. Sixth, Kraemer asked his board to reduce his performance bonus by at least 60 percent and asked his top executives to take pay cuts of 20 percent.

Baxter didn't have to do all this and could easily have fallen into traps that lead to distrust. For instance, it might have blamed Althin's former owners for the problems with the filters. Baxter could also have maintained that there was nothing it could have done to prevent the problem. It might have chosen to keep a low profile, especially because this tragedy occurred around the time of a greater tragedy—the 9/11 attack. With coverage of the attack dominating the news, Baxter could have chosen to say nothing, recognizing that it would receive very little negative publicity. It also probably had a decent legal case and could have chosen to litigate at least some of the lawsuits.

Baxter, though, took the high road. It didn't make the mistakes we've seen other companies make. Baxter people didn't blame others; they didn't withhold information that was important to share; they didn't take a short-term mentality and focus only on how they could limit their financial losses. Instead, they were proactive in their actions and compassionate in their attitudes. Because of this approach, Baxter's stock price wasn't significantly impacted by these problems. Though the renal business suffered in Europe (where many of the deaths occurred), it gained a great deal of trust with its other constituencies. Government regulators, health-care professionals, the media, and employees all seemed to believe that Baxter acted responsibly.

Act #2: Responding to False Accusations

Earlier I noted that situations occur when a company may feel it has done nothing wrong but will appear to be uncaring if it denies responsibility or blames others for the problem. This can turn into a major trust crisis if evidence emerges indicating that the denying company shared some of the blame for the situation (or *appeared* to be responsible). Baxter, for instance, chose to take full responsibility for a problem that may have not been its fault. What was right for Baxter, however, might not be right for another organization if circumstances are different. Companies can be falsely accused, and after an analysis of the situation, believe that evidence will emerge clearing them of any culpability. If they do a cost-benefit analysis and are convinced that they are better off absolving themselves of responsibility, then issuing a complete and unequivocal denial may be the proper trust-building action.

If companies choose this course of action, however, their denial must be thorough and heartfelt. In 1993, the Pepsi-Cola Bottling Co. began hearing the news that syringes had been found in cans of Diet Pepsi in the Seattle area. A few days later, another tampering report surfaced in New Orleans. Claims of tampering started coming in from other cities, and Pepsi immediately formed a crisis management team; its analysis led Pepsi to conclude that these reports were a hoax. Nonetheless, the media had gotten wind of the story. Parallels were drawn to the Tylenol tampering case of a few years earlier. Some retailers began pulling Pepsi products from the shelves, and sales fell off during the height of the crisis.

Pepsi, though, was adamant that this was a hoax, and presented its case to the media. The company filmed the canning process at its Philadelphia plant to demonstrate why it would be impossible for someone working there to slip a syringe into a can. Pepsi showed how if someone were to open a can and place a syringe in it at the point of sale, the tampering would be obvious to any consumer. Craig Weatherup, president of Pepsi-Cola North America, did a taped interview stating Pepsi's position that was distributed by satellite and seen by 165 million people. Weatherup also appeared on many of the major television news programs— *Good Morning America, Larry King Live, Today*—explaining the evidence indicating the syringe scare was a hoax.

After a few days of panic and uncertainty, the tide started turning in Pepsi's favor. The FDA commissioner announced that no tampering report had been confirmed. Shortly thereafter, the police began arresting people who were making false claims about the syringes; others retracted their accusations. It quickly became clear to the media and the public that it was indeed a hoax. Pepsi ran nationwide ads thanking people for having faith in the company and reiterating that the stories of syringes in Pepsi cans were pure fiction. Wisely, Pepsi also ran $1-off coupon ads on cases of Pepsi and gave coupons to employees to distribute to friends and family. Even though Pepsi had been cleared from even the appearance of wrongdoing, the company demonstrated its appreciation for customers sticking with it by offering the coupons.

Sales, which had dropped briefly, quickly picked up and returned to normal. Retailers that had taken the product off their shelves restocked once it was clear that there was no problem. Pepsi emerged from this crisis with its reputation intact and the admiration of the media, the trade, and customers for the speed with which it confronted the issue and for its willingness to provide detailed information.

Act #3: Rebuilding Relationships After Destroying Them

In the early 1990s, highly publicized accusations of racism were made against Denny's Restaurants, and class action lawsuits alleging racism were filed against them. Business fell off because of these events, especially business from minority customers. Denny's, naturally enough, wanted to rebuild relationships with these alienated customers. Typically, companies attempt to rebound from crises of this sort with short-lived, cosmetic efforts. More than one organization accused of racism has responded with token diversity training and pledges to hire more minorities. Although these actions may temporarily reduce the heat, they don't restore trust. Because the root causes of the problem haven't been addressed, racism resurfaces at some later date. It's also possible that these token efforts are viewed cynically by both employees and external stakeholders, and though policies might change, everyone still believes the company harbors the same off-putting values and beliefs.

Denny's, however, did more than respond with token actions. The chain made an extraordinary commitment of time, money, and creativity to foster diversity among corporate and restaurant employees. Though it launched a diversity training program, there was nothing token about it. Everyone in the company participated in it, from board members to restaurant personnel. Though restaurant managers received the most intensive training, the program was designed to impact the entire organization, and at one point more than one hundred certified diversity trainers were on staff.

Denny's efforts didn't stop with this program. A good sign of how committed it was to changing the company was the in-depth analysis of recruitment practices. This analysis revealed that Denny's had been overly dependent on executive recruitment firms that tended to overlook minority candidates. Many of these firms were run by white males who were plugged into the "old boy network." Denny's had worked with these firms for years, and this dependence created a kind of de facto discrimination. For this reason, Denny's began hiring recruitment firms owned by African Americans, Hispanics, and women to supplement hiring needs.

In addition, the company provided incentive to its top managers to change their hiring practices, linking a percentage of senior management bonuses to their ability to hire women and minorities. Denny's also increased its spending with minority suppliers and began donating significant sums of money to civil rights organizations. Finally, the company made a strong effort to attract minority franchisees, and 42 percent of Denny's franchised restaurants are now minority owned.

As a result, a Denny's study showed that black customers increased in the chain's restaurants from 51 million in 1998 to 61 million in 2000, and overall sales have also increased.

Denny's efforts not only rebuilt trust, but they were plain good business. Denny's recognized that it had to implement a multidimensional strategy, addressing "flaws" in the entire system. In this way, it not only corrected the flaws but also communicated a sincere desire to change the way Denny's did business.

Act #4: Doing Good for Society and the Bottom Line

One of the biggest complaints organizational leaders have about charitable contributions is that they are divorced from business strategy. In other words, their good works bear little relationship to what the company is all about. A dot-com contributes millions to the NAACP or a major accounting firm sponsors Greenpeace programs, and everyone from employees to customers is left to wonder what the connection is between the company and its cause. It's difficult to build trust when people don't see a fit between your charitable efforts and your business mission.

Lowe's Home Improvement Warehouse has done a great job in finding that fit. Locked in a battle with Home Depot for leadership in its category, Lowe's has successfully appealed to women shoppers, a market that Home Depot has not pursued as vigorously or as effectively. In targeting this market, Lowe's hasn't simply positioned itself as a store for women do-it-yourselfers. It has taken the sort of actions that prove there's substance behind its positioning. For instance, Lowe's is stocking the type of items— Laura Ashley paints, premium bathroom fixtures, high-end kitchen appliances, and cabinets—that tend to appeal more to women than to men. It also has configured the stores in such a way that there is more aisle room and less clutter than in a typical Home Depot store. These wide aisles certainly must involve a certain sales-per-square-foot sacrifice, but the company gains in less tangible ways.

Lowe's is a strong supporter of the Y-ME National Breast Cancer Organization, providing it with a sizable monetary contribution as well as setting aside space for an in-store awareness display in the fall. The display includes Y-ME brochures and other awareness-building items. In addition, Lowe's runs banner ads for Y-ME on its Web site and refers customers and employees to the site, encouraging personal donations.

Because of these efforts, an astonishing 50 percent of Lowe's customers are women. Just as significantly, Lowe's 2002 sales increased approximately 20 percent over the previous year. Though many factors can be cited for Lowe's success, it has clearly earned the respect and patronage of women customers, and this has made Lowe's a formidable competitor to Home Depot.

Act #5: Making House Calls

Maintaining trust over a sustained period of time is a worthy goal for *all* companies, but it's also a challenging goal. To be consistent about a trust-maintenance strategy in the face of all the things that could cause you to be inconsistent—financial problems, labor issues, lawsuits, and so on—requires great commitment to a way of doing business. One company that has demonstrated this commitment is Snap-on Tools.

A $2 billion company, Snap-on's success revolves around a dealer network that travels in vans to customers' businesses—gas stations, auto repair shops, construction sites, transportation service centers, and so on. The notion of taking its business to the customer rather than having the customer go to it—the vans contain thousands of products—is certainly an innovative way of providing customer service, and Snap-on's ability to maintain this service for more than eighty years has earned it a loyal customer base.

But what really sets Snap-on apart is that it not only has met customer expectations, but it has exceeded them in ways that few companies are able to do. Customers seem to look forward to the arrival of the Snap-on van; people actually leave their work establishments to go outside and wait for the van's arrival. Rather than viewing dealers as people who are trying to sell them something, they see them as providing a valuable service that helps their businesses.

Snap-on has been able to create this type of customer relationship in many different ways. Certainly it has been very proactive in making sure it offers state-of-the-art tools that have great warrantees. Perhaps more significantly, Snap-on was one of the first companies in the industry to extend interest-free credit to customers, allowing even small operations to purchase high-quality tools. This willingness to extend credit—especially considering that many of the customers were small and this was far from standard practice at the time—communicated that it trusted its customers. This trust was returned, and it was greatly beneficial to Snap-on as the small customers became larger ones.

Snap-on also treats its franchise/dealers well. In 2002, it was named the second best home/franchiser by *Entrepreneur* magazine, reflecting the excellent financial deals, support, and training it provides to its dealers. It's one thing to have employees build strong relationships with customers. Franchisees, though, are one step removed from the corporation. Motivating these dealers to represent the company's values and beliefs can be a challenge. Snap-on, however, has met this challenge year after year. It has recognized that you can't build trust only on the back of a solid brand (which it has). Early on, Snap-on grasped that if the company treated dealers with care and consideration, it would impact how the dealers treated customers.

Act #6: Helping People Up After a Downsizing

By the very act itself, downsizing is a betrayal of trust. It communicates to employees that the organization's strategy has failed; that management has somehow messed up and the employees are the ones who have to pay. It's not surprising, therefore, that a significant downsizing creates tremendous animosity toward the organization, both among the employees who are let go as well as their coworkers who escape the ax but resent that their friends are being fired (and often worry that they're going to be next).

In 2001, Agilent Technologies had to let go a total of eight thousand people (in two waves of four thousand each) because of a slump in the industry. Customers canceled $250 million in orders in one quarter alone, and the company had no choice but to cut back. Still, after cutting costs everywhere it could, Agilent had to downsize. Some companies downsize in a bureaucratic, emotionally neutral manner. In many instances, employees of public companies learn of the downsizing from the media after the company has informed financial analysts. Sometimes, top management distances itself from the actual process of letting people go.

None of this happened at Agilent. Instead, the CEO, Bill Barnholt, went on the company's public address system and announced the first downsizing. Speaking emotionally about how difficult it was for him to make this decision, he detailed how the process would work and provided as many details as he could. Only after making this internal announcement did he release this information to analysts and the media.

Next, Agilent put three thousand managers through training sessions to help them understand how to let people go in the most humane way possible. The company also emphasized to these managers that they should be as open as possible in the weeks before the downsizing took place, answering everyone's questions and taking the time to explain how the decision about who to downsize would be made. To that end, the criteria for this decision were posted on Agilent's intranet site.

Less than a year after the first four thousand people were fired, management decided that another four thousand people had to go. The training and information program was repeated. Certainly people were upset and angry. But amazingly, many employees expressed appreciation for Agilent's honesty and the way it tried to make the process as painless as possible. For instance, Agilent decided to shut down one of its chip-manufacturing groups and transfer a small percentage of that office's employees to another location in order to save millions of dollars; the rest of the employees would be fired within the year. When the announcement was made, chip production fell precipitously. And then, it began to improve. In fact, Agilent soon was producing chips at a record pace, exceeding everyone's expectations. Though you could argue that people were trying to demonstrate how valuable they were in the faint hope that their jobs would be saved, it seems more likely that they were responding positively to the company's fairness and honesty. Even though the employees were upset about losing their jobs, they must have recognized that Agilent had no alternative and was handling the situation with the employees' needs in mind.

Act #7: Treating Employees Like Family

This is the great cliché of American business: We treat our employees like family. In reality, business sometimes treats them like poor relations. Although CEOs may sincerely want to show the same compassion and caring toward their employees as they do toward real family members, this is often not possible. Mailroom personnel aren't treated the same as vice presidents. Salaries and perks are wildly different. Executives have much more influence and personal freedom than clerical workers.

Yet the impulse to treat employees like family is a good one; it helps build loyalty and commitment. The challenge for companies is to overcome the inherent inequities in any business and create a true family atmosphere.

Motek is a small software company (fewer than one hundred employees) that monitors the movement of merchandise in warehouses. It has demonstrated the creativity I mentioned earlier, creating a family atmosphere through innovative benefits programs, policies, and compensation approaches, including:

- Everyone at the company receives five weeks of vacation.

- Houses or condos purchased in the neighborhood (Beverly Hills) are subsidized by Motek.

- Employees are given a leased luxury car after ten years with the company.

- People are invited to join in meetings even if they're not part of a given functional group.

- Teams decide what they're going to work on in a given week (rather than receiving assignments from management).

- When work on a project clearly isn't going to meet a deadline, the individual responsible receives a small monetary bonus if he informs the group early enough (so more people can be put on the project or other remedial steps can be taken with time to spare).

- Everyone receives one of three pay levels (between $30,000 and $70,000) except for two employees.

- Each founding employee will receive one percent of Motek's value when it's sold.

In short, employees are treated with great respect and receive meaningful perks. Equality is put into action at Motek, and people feel empowered. Employees willingly accept lower-than-normal salaries in exchange for being treated fairly and for sharing in the profits when the company does well. In fact, the CEO's promise of one percent value when the company is sold is purely verbal. Employees trust the CEO to the point that they don't need the promise in writing.

Motek can treat people like family in part because it's a small, private company. Obviously, it would be impossible for a Fortune 500 company to do some of the things that Motek has done. On the other hand, larger organizations can take a cue from Motek. They can be inspired to be more creative in the way they build relationships with their people. If a company truly believes its employees are family, it has to be ready to demonstrate this belief through policies and programs. Although most organizations are unable to subsidize housing for their people or give them one percent of the company, they can come up with other original approaches that communicate how much they respect and value their employees.

Act #8: Communicating That You Care

Countless numbers of organizations talk about themselves as "caring companies," yet many times it's just talk. Though they make charitable contributions and pay competitive salaries, they also are myopically focused on results. It's transparently clear to employees and other stakeholders that these companies do not put their people first, no matter what they might say. In other instances, organizations really do care, but they're not particularly skilled at showing their empathy and compassion. They lack the innovative programs and media savvy that demonstrates they're humanistic organizations.

Pfizer Pharmaceuticals doesn't suffer from these problems. On all levels, Pfizer has exhibited great empathy and concern for others. At a time when drug companies have received their share of negative publicity, Pfizer has managed to maintain its highly trusted brand and its reputation as a great place to work. According to *The Chronicle of Philanthropy*, Pfizer donated more to foundations and not-for-profit groups than any other corporation in 2000. Its $340,514,019 total was significantly more than the next highest contributor, Merck & Co., which gave $249,000,000.

Just being a large corporate giver, though, isn't enough to achieve trust strategy goals. Pfizer has implemented care-focused activities in a variety of areas. For instance, its "Sharing the Care" and "Connection to Care" programs provide medications to people who otherwise couldn't afford them, giving well over $100 million worth of pharmaceuticals to uninsured and low-income people.

In addition, Pfizer dedicates tremendous time and resources to developing its people, spending 14 percent of its payroll on workforce development programs. Rarely outsourcing training, Pfizer is willing to make this significant expenditure in order to help people develop the skills, knowledge, and values that are critical to the company.

Finally, Pfizer's CEO, Hank McKinnell, is the type of leader who does a terrific job of communicating the company's values. He doesn't leave this job to others. Instead, through his direct involvement in charitable activities and through his highly employee-centric policies, he is well-known as a leader who values integrity and compassion. He is also able and willing to articulate these values eloquently in speeches and media interviews.

What These Acts Have in Common

Although these trust-building acts involved different situations and issues, they have certain things in common. CEOs were often visibly involved in implementing programs and policies. Companies took risks and exercised creativity to solve problems and meet stakeholder needs. Leaders acted out of a sincere desire to assist stakeholders first, placing other requirements second. The courses of action generally were multidimensional; the concerns of the media, employees, customers, and other groups were fully addressed.

Now that I've offered these inspiring stories of trust building, I'd like to share some cautionary tales of companies that made trust-building mistakes.

12

Acts of Distrust

It is much easier to be critical than to be correct.

—BENJAMIN DISRAELI

Most of us are aware of how a relatively small number of companies lost trust quickly, dramatically, and devastatingly. Enron, Arthur Andersen, Exxon, WorldCom, and United Airlines are just some of these companies. Through unethical practices, poor judgment, or plain, old-fashioned greed, they made mistakes that alienated their stakeholders. Organizations, however, can lose trust in a slower, more private manner, though sometimes no less devastatingly. I'd like to share some examples of how this can happen.

These examples are purposefully diverse, chosen to demonstrate that actions creating distrust can happen in all sorts of ways in all types of organizations. As you'll see, they're not always the result of one calamitous miscalculation. Sometimes distrust is built incrementally and insidiously, the consequence of a culture where results are all that matter. In other instances, it is the product of arrogance, where one or more organizational leaders fail to take the concerns of customers or employees or other groups into consideration.

I also want to stress that these examples are not cited to indict the organizations as a whole. My focus is on *specific* acts of distrust. A company may have made a single mistake that is a blemish on an otherwise spotless record. It's also possible that the mistake was related to a specific time, place, or individual, and that some organizations in that position would have done the same thing. And it may be that since the distrust-building incident occurred, these companies have made a comeback and proved themselves to have stellar values and great stakeholder relationships.

Therefore, think about the acts themselves and how they serve as cautionary lessons for what can happen when issues of trust aren't fully considered.

Act #1: Making a Difficult Leadership Transition Even More Difficult

When brilliant, charismatic CEOs leave companies, it's often inevitable that their companies experience second-guessing and morale problems. People like Ralph Larsen and Lee Iacocca are hard acts to follow, not only because they were strong leaders but because they established reputations for integrity and relationship building that others can't match immediately. To a certain extent, the new CEOs need to develop thick skin. If they overreact to criticism or decide to implement their own strategies out of egotism (because they want to prove they can blaze a path as bright and shining as their predecessors), they risk breaking the bonds with stakeholders the company has worked hard to build.

Under Stanley Gault's leadership in the 1980s, Rubbermaid stock kept going up, sales were terrific, and the company received numerous accolades from the media for being well managed as well as a great place to work. When Gault left in 1991, the numbers dropped and complaints from retailers began rolling in. These complaints involved slow shipping, an inability to ship as much as retailers wanted, and high prices. As problems mounted, Rubbermaid responded with:

- Two major restructurings that alienated many employees and helped accelerate the exodus of managerial talent

- Overly optimistic earnings forecasts that weren't met (this happened more than once) and rubbed analysts and shareholders the wrong way

- A failure to take full responsibility for its financial problems, blaming high raw-material prices and at one point attempting to pass costs on to retailers

Rubbermaid managed to hurt relationships with employees, analysts, shareholders, and retailers. Instead of attempting to strengthen the trust built during Gault's tenure, it allowed relationships to deteriorate. Perhaps the new management team was overly concerned about short-term performance or was simply trying to deal with market changes that didn't exist when Gault was CEO. Though it's a mistake to attribute Rubbermaid's slide exclusively to Gault's departure, it seems that the company forgot what made Rubbermaid such a terrific organization. Instead of nurturing relationships that were critical to the company, management seemed to have taken at least some of them for granted.

Act #2: Underestimating the Impact of Unethical Behavior

In a cynical, jaded age, people often fail to realize that most of us retain the capacity to be shocked by bad behavior. President

Clinton's dalliances, the machinations of Arthur Andersen audi-
tors, and the greed of highly compensated CEOs whose companies go bankrupt outrage many people. Organizations frequently
overestimate how much we're willing to let them get away with.
They don't seem to realize that their own employees as well as
external communities will be highly offended by questionable or
unethical behavior, and that unless they address this problem
quickly and decisively, trust will be lost.

When Suzy Wetlaufer, an editor at the *Harvard Business Review*, became romantically involved with former General Electric
head Jack Welch, she was also working on an interview with Welch
for the *Review*. Clearly, this was a conflict of interest, but the magazine decided that it had too much invested in the interview to
kill it; it had publicized the interview, and Welch was a great catch
(for the magazine, if not for Ms. Wetlaufer). As a result, the magazine's editorial director asked two other editors to revise the interview.

A number of editors called for Wetlaufer's resignation, but she
neither resigned nor was fired. Arguments raged internally about
the appropriateness of allowing Wetlaufer to stay on and of pub-
lishing the interview. Soon other media picked up on the story,
and the debate about the magazine's actions went public. This
increased the pressure on the journal and a few months later the
Review announced that Wetlaufer would have a new position as
editor at large and retain her office. Although the magazine may
have considered this "demotion" from her previous editorial post
as appropriate punishment for her sins, many *Review* staffers
didn't agree. Two senior editors resigned in protest, and one of
them said, "I didn't resign because of Suzy and Jack, I resigned
because I lost faith in *Harvard Business Review*'s ability to do the
right thing."

These resignations created even more negative publicity, especially when it came out that Welch had helped structure Wet-

laufer's new deal as editor at large. Eventually, Wetlaufer resigned, but the damage had been done.

Clearly, this affair spiraled out of control. If Wetlaufer had been asked to resign and if the interview had been killed immediately, employees as well as readers would not have lost trust in management's judgment. It's ironic that *Harvard Business Review*, the paragon of managerial wisdom, would make this mistake, but it's also instructive. The magazine (like many organizations facing ethical dilemmas) seems to have had difficulty gaining an objective perspective on the situation. At the beginning, the publication's management group probably couldn't imagine that some of its people would resign and that it would receive so much negative publicity and criticism from other publications and readers. They underestimated how strongly people would react to what was perceived as an unethical action.

It's also important to note that Wetlaufer was considered a top editor who had helped the *Review* enormously during her tenure. Her bosses must have viewed her as a highly productive, valuable employee and wanted to avoid losing her. As I've alluded to earlier, companies often have to decide whether to keep top performers who behave in ways that hurt the company's reputation or lower employee morale. It's all too easy to weigh the tangible contributions of a high performer against the intangible damage of a loss of trust and vote for the tangible contributions. As the *Review* learned, this is not the best choice in the long run.

Act #3: Failing to Anticipate Trust Vulnerabilities

As we've seen, a loss of trust isn't always the result of a company's misdeeds. In fact, most companies are not guilty of Enron-like greed and malfeasance. Instead, their sins are more subtle. Too often, they simply overlook how their actions impact a particular group's trust (or lack thereof) in the organization. Instead of pursuing a trust bank strategy where they look for opportunities to build and solidify stakeholder relationships, companies unwittingly fall into trust-breaking traps.

During the 1996 Olympics in Atlanta, IBM provided a mammoth, multipurpose computer system that, among other things, relayed contest results to the media, established an Internet site specifically for Atlanta visitors, and had IBM terminals located throughout the Olympics area loaded with all types of information. Almost immediately after the Olympics began, problems cropped up with the system. Most significantly, the media received incorrect information about results and athletes, including bizarre things such as a fencing contestant winning a track event and the description of one Olympic participant as being two feet tall. Results also came in very slowly, frustrating reporters trying to meet deadlines. In addition, reporters complained that too few terminals were available for media use exclusively.

Angry reporters criticized IBM on the air and in their stories, resulting in highly unfavorable publicity. Just as significantly, IBM had invited twenty-five hundred major customers to Atlanta to view the technology, and it suffered the embarrassment of having these customers witness the system's glitches.

In one sense, IBM did nothing wrong. Most of the technical problems, in fact, could be traced to factors beyond its control. For instance, the Atlanta Committee for the Olympic Games rather than IBM was directly responsible for providing the media with news from the Games. In addition, IBM had to integrate its services with other technology providers such as AT&T and Motorola.

The bigger issue, though, was that IBM didn't seem to anticipate the negative impact if anything went wrong and that it, rather than anyone else, would receive the lion's share of the blame. IBM never insisted that its system undergo a comprehensive test before the Olympics. If it had, it would have discovered that the news agency partners were using "slow" modems that couldn't deliver results to reporters on a timely basis.

With hindsight, IBM should have done everything possible to reduce the number of foul-ups. By recognizing the potential for both building trust and diminishing it at this event, IBM might have taken Murphy's Law to heart: If something can go wrong, it will go wrong. Although IBM may have been unable to prevent certain problems, it probably could have eliminated others (and perhaps reduced the severity of the problems that did occur).

Act #4: Appearing Like You're Not Playing by the Rules

When companies are perceived as underhanded or arrogant, they lose respect. For instance, they bully suppliers into lowering their prices or they use their influence with government to get a favorable tax law passed. When large, powerful corporations act in this manner, they send the message that "the rules don't apply to us." This may not be their intent—and they actually may be operating in a fair and equitable manner—but the perception is that they're taking advantage of others. This perception tarnishes the company's reputation and strains relationships.

Oracle Corporation is one of the country's most successful software companies, run by founder and CEO Larry Ellison, who has alternately been described as brilliant and arrogant in media profiles. Like most software companies, it has been hit hard by the industry slump that started in 2000, and Oracle's stock has lost a great deal of its value. The company has lost a number of top executives as well as some customers to competitors. Though Oracle has a strong product line and will undoubtedly recover from its problems, it's possible these problems would have had less impact if the company had countered negative perceptions about how it operates.

One event that fostered these perceptions took place in 1999, when Oracle hired a private investigation firm to look into how Microsoft operated. According to press reports, the firm examined the contents of dumpsters used by trade associations that had good relationships with Microsoft. When these reports surfaced, Ellison responded that he didn't see anything wrong with what Oracle did and viewed it as a "public service." Though Oracle may have felt it was doing the right thing—Oracle as well as other companies like Netscape and Sun Microsystems were complaining about Microsoft's business practices—the perception in some quarters was different. It's quite possible that the government's investigation of Microsoft was spurred in part by Silicon Valley competitors' complaints, and this perception didn't reflect well on Oracle.

A year later, Oracle began selling its 11i business suite software, and customers who bought it complained that it contained bugs. Industry speculation was that Oracle had shipped the product knowing it might have some glitches but felt it couldn't delay its rollout any longer. As customers continued to complain, Ellison didn't issue an apology. Instead, at one trade conference he gave a talk in which he suggested customers may have caused the problems by tinkering with the software.

None of the things Oracle did were catastrophic. None of them created a major crisis. Nonetheless, the perception it created with its attitudes and actions weakened relationships. Though it's impossible to know how much it was weakened, Oracle's reputation was tarnished, and the impact of that tarnished reputation may be felt in the coming years.

Act #5: Appearing Like You Have Something to Hide

Companies can create distrust not just by what they say but by what they don't say. There are instances when silence speaks vol-

umes. For example, a company's fortunes go south and weeks or
months go by without it saying anything about the possibility of
downsizing until employees read about planned massive layoffs
in the papers. Or a class action discrimination lawsuit is filed
against an organization and a company refuses to comment on
it, even as rumors circulate about the company's terribly discriminatory policies. An unwillingness to clarify a situation or defend
the company against charges tends to weaken the bonds of trust.

America Online (AOL) grew by leaps and bounds in a relatively short period of time and then became part of media empire
Time Warner. Given its cutting-edge technology, leadership position in its industry, huge membership, and potential synergies
with Time Warner units, AOL should be a favorite of Wall Street.
In fact, Wall Street has voiced skepticism about AOL over the
years. Much of this skepticism involves issues of full financial disclosure. For years, analysts have questioned the revenue figures
provided by AOL. Specifically, they called on AOL to give them
specific breakdowns of revenues in categories such as commis-
sions, advertising backlog, and so on.

Some analysts suspected that AOL's stated revenues have provided an overly rosy picture of the company's financial health.
For a long time, analysts have questioned how Internet companies can make money, concerned that they lacked viable business
strategies. To diminish or eliminate this skepticism, AOL could
have provided analysts with detailed responses to their questions.
Although AOL has been more forthcoming in recent years, it still
has not satisfied a number of critics in the financial community.
A series of *Washington Post* articles in 2001 implied that AOL's
advertising revenues might be overstated. The articles suggested
that a percentage of this revenue was the result of barter arrangements and investments in dot-coms where in return for the investments, dot-coms advertise on AOL. The revenue received

from these arrangements may inflate the total revenue figures unfairly, or so the *Post* articles alleged.

AOL has been accused of being evasive about the numbers,
and it's possible this evasiveness is rooted in strategic concerns or
fears that analysts will misinterpret the results from a financially
complex business. Whatever the reason, AOL would be in a much
stronger position if it could establish more open, trusting relationships with the financial community, and this isn't going to
happen until it does a better job of communicating with this community.

Act #6: Refusing to Face Reality

Some organizations are too proud for their own good. They are
very successful for a period of time, but they can't adjust to
changes in the marketplace that demand they adapt how they
operate. As a result, they stubbornly—some might say, obsessively—follow a path that everyone, from their employees to the
financial community and from their vendors to their customers,
knows is wrong. Trust is lost because when companies aren't honest with themselves, they're not honest with others.

From 1984 to 1992, Waste Management was one of the top-
performing companies in the world. It grew with incredible speed
and success, acquiring other companies and branching out into
myriad areas, including hazardous waste disposal, recycling, and
water treatment. Everything the company touched seemed to
turn to gold. Eventually, of course, things changed. It overpaid for
acquisitions, and the waste management industry experienced a
decline. It became a big, bloated company, but no one could face
this truth. Instead, it adhered to an expansion strategy that made
a bad situation worse.

No doubt, some managers recognized that this was the wrong
strategy. One, a finance director, suggested that cost cutting was

essential, but his recommendations were ignored. The company kept making highly optimistic financial forecasts that weren't met and putting money in businesses that weren't profitable. It was on a downhill slide that perhaps could have been stopped, but the company's hubris got in the way. If Waste Management would have cut costs, offered more realistic financial forecasts, and focused on its core business, it might have strengthened the relationships it needed to survive. Instead, the company strained these relationships. For instance, Waste Management had spurned merger offers with royal disdain, acting as if it was still king of the hill. It's quite possible that if the company had not alienated potential merger partners, one of them might have suggested a deal that would have worked.

Instead, Waste Management sank further and began inflating its numbers to maintain the illusion that it was still a viable entity. Ultimately, it announced a pretax charge of $3.5 billion because of its accounting methods (Arthur Andersen was its auditor), the Securities and Exchange Commission launched an investigation, and the company was sold to a much smaller competitor.

Act #7: Changing Too Much Too Fast

Change has been embraced by the corporate world, and organizations have changed policies, processes, and even cultures to fit new realities. In many instances, this has helped organizations become more successful and more responsive to employees' needs. In some situations, though, change has trampled corporate traditions and left employees, customers, and other groups confused about mission and values. At its worst, radical change can plunge a company into a type of limbo, where it's neither the company it was nor the company it wants to be. In other words, people aren't sure what the company is, and it's difficult to trust an entity without an identity.

Kmart's bankruptcy in 2002 can be attributed to many factors, but with hindsight, it seems that management's eagerness to transform the company as quickly as possible was a factor in its downfall. Kmart's board of directors brought in a new CEO, Chuck Conaway, a little less than two years before it declared bankruptcy. At the time, the board recognized that change was necessary and hired Conaway because he was the type of young, aggressive leader who seemed best suited to lead a change strategy. Conaway, in turn, brought in his own cadre of young, aggressive executives who were eager to do battle with Wal-Mart.

When Conaway took over, he quickly had the portraits of his predecessors removed from his office and the company auditorium. He also ordered the removal of a large bronze sculpture in front of corporate headquarters. Both these moves clearly communicated that things were going to change. One of the most significant changes was updating Kmart's old distribution and inventory control systems as well as sprucing up the look of outdated stores. No doubt, this was the right thing to do, but Kmart spent $2 billion on fixing the distribution and inventory control systems. In addition, Conaway and his newly hired executives traveled from store to store attempting to remedy Kmart's customer service problems with direct intervention. According to a number of accounts, the new Kmart leadership team was perceived by some store managers as arrogant. Kmart, after all, was a one-hundred-year-old company, and many of the store managers had been with the company for a long time. They resented being told how to run their stores by newcomers. As a result, some store managers either resigned or were fired.

Then Kmart launched a price war, asking customers to compare Kmart's prices with those at competitors Wal-Mart and Target. Again, this may have been a good strategy if implemented correctly. But this massive decrease in prices cut into store profits and wasn't something Kmart could sustain. Traditionally, it had driven customers into their stores through promotional advertising, and the combination of advertising costs and lowered prices hurt.

Kmart's bankruptcy had a lot to do with excessive spending and declining revenues, but the trust factor also played a role. When a company is one hundred years old, it establishes a culture and business practices that can't be changed overnight. When an attempt was made to change them almost this quickly, the moves alienated employees and confused customers. Conaway had the ambitious goal of challenging Wal-Mart for industry leadership, and he certainly had some bold ideas for doing so. But everything happened too fast, suppliers lost faith in the company's ability to pay its bills, and bankruptcy claimed yet another major corporation.

Act #8: Putting the Company's Needs Before Those of the Customer

One of the fastest ways to lose trust is by prioritizing the company's requirements over those of the customers and making it clear to customers that they come in second. Typically, this sin is committed because of organizational arrogance. A company believes its product or service is so much better than anything else out there that it can raise prices, reduce services, and make other changes that benefit it and don't benefit customers. Although some companies may be able to get away with these actions in the short term, in the long term they suffer because they won't always have competitive advantage. Eventually, other companies will catch up with them and customers will eagerly shift their loyalties because of the way they've been treated.

TurboTax, manufactured by Intuit Inc., is the leader in personal income tax software and by all accounts a superior software package. The company decided to install an antipiracy device in the latest version of TurboTax. This device involved product activation technology, allowing people to use the software only on the computer that it was originally installed on. This angered users for a number of reasons. First, it prevented them from using TurboTax on any of their other computers or if they installed a new hard drive. Second, the product activation part of the product runs continuously, using up part of the computer's memory. Third, users who have "spyware" detectors on their machines are warned that confidential data is being extracted while the product activation technology is on (though Intuit has convincingly denied this is the case).

As a result, Intuit received an avalanche of customer complaints. Just as tellingly, this copy protection attempt created a great deal of buzz on the Internet; one person went so far as to create a Web site designed to encourage a boycott of TurboTax products.

To its credit, Intuit has issued statements that it intends to fix the problems with TurboTax and has backed that up with new product development efforts. Still, the company is now in the position of having to rebuild trust rather than maintain it, a position it should never have placed itself in.

What We Can Learn from These Acts

Even the world's leading companies commit acts that create distrust. IBM, Oracle, and America Online are premier organizations that for a variety of reasons hurt their relationships and reputations. The point: Losing trust can happen to anyone. These three organizations are top-performing companies that are well regarded by the majority of internal and external groups. If they can slip up, anyone can. Though these three organizations didn't suffer the same fate as Kmart or Waste Management, the episodes described created chinks in their armor. It made people reassess their opinion of these companies. It planted the seed of doubt that these companies were as trustworthy as they had previously seemed.

In a very real way, each episode served as a withdrawal from the company's trust bank. At some point in the future, this withdrawal may hurt companies. If they're facing a crisis of a greater magnitude at that point, the earlier incident may work against them. It may cause a top employee to decide to look elsewhere for work or a customer to choose a competitor.

When a company does something that diminishes trust, the consequences can be major or minor, short-term or long-term. Just because it doesn't lead to an immediate bankruptcy doesn't mean that it won't have an impact. It pays for all organizations to be *exceptionally* vigilant against committing acts of distrust.

CHAPTER 13

The Ten Commandments of Organizational Trust

I've searched all the parks in all the cities—and found no statues of Committees.

—G. K. CHESTERTON

At this point, I hope you've acquired the knowledge and motivation necessary to increase the level of trust your organization receives. Though this is by no means an easy task, it is a realistic goal. Every company, no matter what its history might be or what its current situation is, can improve its reputation and relationships. Every organization is capable of transforming the suspicions and cynicism of a given audience into trust.

It takes both knowledge and motivation to do so. This isn't something you can wing. You need a plan that's rooted in your company's current needs. Obviously, your plan is going to be different if you've just suffered a devastating, trust-destroying blow than if you're attempting to create a trust bank. For this reason, I've provided you with a wide variety of ideas and tools for putting a trust strategy into action. This knowledge will facilitate your efforts.

At the same time, you also need motivation to put this knowledge to work. It's easy to get sidetracked and put trust-building activities on the backburner. I know more than one organization that decided it didn't have enough money in its budget for these activities or determined it lacked the time and people required. Or it assigned trust-related projects such a low priority that they were forgotten. The many examples and anecdotes I've included were designed to offer motivation. They demonstrate the enormous benefits for organizations that make a firm and continuous commitment to trust building. They also show how resilient companies can be after an incident that makes stakeholders question or even doubt their intentions.

To keep your motivation strong and to put your knowledge to work, I'd like to leave you with what I refer to as the ten commandments of organizational trust. As your company attempts to mend fences, strengthen relationships, and build trusted brands, the following commandments will guide your efforts.

1. Focus on Building Trust First and Restoring It Second

Don't take the wrong message away from this book. Although companies can rebuild relationships that have been damaged by everything from product safety problems to financial scandals, it's much easier to achieve the long-term objective of building trust incrementally year after year. In other words, don't take false reassurance from the fact that it's *possible* to restore trust. Some organizations don't fret over declining employee morale or increasing customer service complaints if business is good, figuring that they can always repair the damage. Perhaps they can, but it will take a far greater commitment in terms of resources than an ongoing trust strategy.

A good analogy is to preventative medicine. It's much easier (not to mention less costly) to take steps to prevent disease than it is to try to cure a disease once it surfaces. Continuing the metaphor, the trust bank concept is very similar to preventative medicine. The problem, of course, is that it's sometimes difficult to see the value of eating fruits and vegetables or of doing good things for internal and external stakeholders. The payoff isn't always immediate or obvious. What I hope you've learned, though, is to take it on faith that there will be a payoff and it will be *significant*.

2. Hold Leadership Accountable for Trust-Building Efforts

One of the biggest mistakes companies can make is assigning responsibility for trust-related activities to a middle-level human resources or communications department employee. It's great to get HR or communications people involved in the process, but it's too big a task for one person to handle, especially if that person isn't in a leadership position. Ideally, the CEO, the board of directors, and a chief trust officer (CTO) will all work together to make a trust strategy happen. For the CEO, this means more than just devoting time to appearing at charity functions or making announcements about new employee benefits policies. The CEO must demonstrate that this is a top priority for him. When a CEO does this, others in the company automatically make it a top priority.

The quote I used to lead off this chapter illustrates that one person ultimately has to make this commitment and set the right tone for the organization. If you'll recall, CEOs like J&J's Ralph Larsen and Deere's Robert Lane spent over 75 percent of their time on communication responsibilities. This is commitment. In fact, some of our most admired U.S. presidents, such as Lincoln, FDR, Truman, and Reagan, had one thing in common: an ability to communicate to our nation when we needed communication most.

Holding CEOs accountable for communicating seems natural, but it's often overlooked. Similarly, most companies lack a CTO who could help ensure this accountability. A company without a CTO often lacks sensitivity to issues of trust. A CTO has her radar up and on all the time and is able to spot problems and opportunities that others might miss. Conceivably, the CTO can spot a crisis that's brewing and alert the organization to the potential problem. She also should be able to see how enacting a given policy may solidify relationships with employees or spot a way in which the CEO can establish greater trust with a key member of the media.

Finally, boards of directors must be truly independent and take on oversight responsibility for implementation of trust programs. In the past, cronyism between CEOs and their boards frequently made this oversight role impossible. Fortunately, most companies are moving away from the traditional buddy-buddy relationship between boards and CEOs. Boards, too, have become much more sensitive to the issue of public trust. In fact, no less a group than the Conference Board formed a "Commission on Public Trust and Private Enterprise," issuing recommendations in early 2003 that included boards "focusing on the corporation's long-term success." If boards could reduce the pressure CEOs feel to satisfy quarterly results requirements, they would make it much easier for companies to take actions that meet the needs of all their stakeholders and not just those of Wall Street.

3. Make Trust Bank Deposits Even If You're the Most Ethical Company in the World

Just as you wouldn't go without health insurance because you're physically fit, you shouldn't go without a trust bank just because your organization has good values. Making regular trust bank deposits is, in fact, great insurance. Unfortunately, some companies believe that they don't need insurance because they enjoy stellar reputations and relationships.

What these companies don't realize is that these reputations and relationships can be destroyed with frightening speed in volatile environments. In an unpredictable, fast-paced society, problems can emerge seemingly out of nowhere and catch companies unawares. Who would have thought that someone would sue an organization because its food products allegedly cause children to become fat? Even though this particular lawsuit was thrown out, it created a perception that was harmful. In our transparent age, news of this lawsuit spread quickly and broadly. Everyone heard about it, and the negative buzz damaged relationships. Complacency, therefore, makes even the most value-conscious companies vulnerable to these types of events.

In other instances, organizations believe they're highly humanistic but possess a "moral" weakness. These companies may have solid values, but they don't apply these values consistently in some work area. They treat their customers well but don't do as good a job with employees. Or they are highly ethical when it comes to financial matters but are rather cutthroat when it comes to competitors. These organizations tend to focus on their ethical behaviors and rationalize the actions that cause relationship problems. Though they see themselves as value-conscious, caring companies, the fact is that they possess an Achilles heel.

Whether you're 100 percent pure or just 90 percent, trust bank deposits will serve you well when an unexpected crisis or problem hits.

4. Do the Right Thing Because It's the Right Thing to Do

I apologize for the Zen-like quality of this commandment, but what it means is that building trust isn't just for show. If you just go through the motions—giving money to a charity because you feel it's expected of your organization or offering employees a new perk because you've been pressured to do so—you're not going to reap the benefits. When your trust-related actions seem self-serving, a response to pressure, or superficial, then they won't do your company much good. People are amazingly perceptive about these sorts of things. They know when a leader really cares about his people versus when he's pretending to care. The commitment and honesty of both an individual and an organization are easy to read and difficult to fake.

Warren Buffett is the type of leader who acts based on his firmly held beliefs. Though many of his actions illustrate this point, his "Berkshire Hathaway Shareholders Report" from February 2002 is a great example. In the report, he levels with shareholders about mistakes made and takes responsibility for these mistakes. Rather than sugarcoat negative news or focus only on the great future ahead, Buffett writes, "Though our corporate performance last year was satisfactory, *my* performance was anything but. I manage most of Berkshire's equity portfolio, and my results were poor. . . ." He then goes on to criticize corporate leaders who prosper while shareholders suffer because of falling stock prices: "But (we) can promise that your economic result from Berkshire will parallel ours during the period of your ownership: We will not take cash compensation, restricted stock or option grants that would make our results superior to yours. Additionally, I will keep well over 99 percent of my net worth in Berkshire. My wife and I have never sold a share nor do we intend to. . . ."

Reading this report, you sense Buffett's commitment to acting in a fair and ethical way, that he's driven by his values as much as his desire for strong performance. Clearly, he is the type of leader who takes great satisfaction in doing the right thing.

Customers want to do business with good people. Employees want to work for good leaders. When leadership is sincere about using resources to benefit employees, customers, the community, and other groups, it attracts the right sort of people. For this reason, companies should attempt to hire individuals with a strong moral sense, compassion, and communication skills whenever possible. Certainly these individuals have to deliver results; nice guys do finish last if they don't perform. But the people who produce results and have solid values possess an unbeatable combination.

This is an especially important commandment for internal use. From CEOs to mailroom workers, people like to feel that they're making a contribution above and beyond just doing job-related tasks. Someone once asked me what made me feel good about my life, and I said that it's when I run into a former employee at a store or a movie and they tell me that they really enjoyed working for my company, that we treated people right, and that we got them involved with activities that balanced community involvement and work.

Organizations can help their employees live more productive, meaningful lives, and organizations that fail to do so are shirking an important responsibility.

5. Practice Humility Even When You Have Plenty to Brag About

The danger of arrogance is that it blinds you to the need for maintaining trusting relationships with stakeholders. Earlier I noted that complacency makes companies vulnerable, and arrogance creates another form of complacency. When a company's sales and earnings are good, when it's expanding, when it's receiving favorable publicity, it sometimes labors under the illusion that it can do no wrong. In these circumstances, even humble CEOs can become arrogant, failing to devote enough attention to problems that can alienate various constituencies. They assume that nothing can seriously hurt the company when it's flying so high, and for a while, they may be right. Ultimately, however, the situation changes and they are hurt.

When everyone is telling you that your company is great, and flattering profiles appear in big business publications, it takes a conscious effort to maintain a certain amount of humility. I'm not suggesting that leaders of these companies never take credit for accomplishments or become unnaturally meek and unassertive. Instead, they simply need to remind themselves that excessive pride goeth before a fall. As proud as they are of their company's accomplishments, they need to keep a tight rein on that pride.

I've known many CEOs of major corporations, and the majority of them possessed a certain measure of humility. They gave credit to others when it was due and acknowledged the luck involved in their own success. They were gracious in victory. In this way, they guarded against the attitudes and behaviors that lead to distrust.

6. Base Your Actions on Principles as Much as on Results

Admittedly, this can be a difficult balance. It tends to be easier to achieve for older organizations with history and tradition to draw upon. It's not a coincidence that Johnson & Johnson, Gerber, Kellogg, and McDonald's are highly trusted companies that have consistently been market leaders. They have established values-based cultures to guide their decision making. It's not unusual for them to ask themselves: Is this action consistent with what we believe in as a company?

Younger companies without a values-rich tradition are less likely to ask this question. They often are operating purely in the present, making decisions only on current realities rather than weighing these decisions against what the company stands for.

This doesn't mean that younger companies will automatically place results over values. It obviously depends on who their leaders are and what they believe. Still, I've seen young, fast-growth companies that are especially vulnerable to acting first and considering the value implications later. They become so caught up in pursuing fast-growth strategies that they don't have the time or perspective to consider the larger implications of their actions.

Older companies, of course, aren't guaranteed anything just because they have the benefit of a solid tradition. Recently, I met with the head of a fifty-year-old company, and this CEO talked about how he felt the company had lost its way because it had forsaken some of the principles of its founder. As he was reciting some of these principles to me, they sounded a bit corny. Yet at the same time, they embodied a belief in honesty and fair play that had been discarded as this company grew and moved from private to public. Listening to this CEO, I found it admirable that he wanted to restore these principles and hoped that he would be able to strike a balance with the need for results.

7. Avoid Shortcuts

This commandment really means rejecting a win-at-all-costs attitude. You would think that today's leaders would have a kinder, gentler approach than those raised in the old school, militaristic style. Although it's true that there aren't as many CEOs today who bark orders and treat employees like privates in their own personal army, just as many CEOs are driven by ego and ambition. Executives of all types are willing to cross an ethical line in order to achieve better results. They're willing to lie to employees in order to retain key people. They're willing to misstate earnings in order to please analysts. They're willing to lower quality standards in order to increase profits. On a smaller scale, executives will manipulate their direct reports, say anything to customers in order to please them, and be willing to stab someone in the back in order to make themselves look better.

Trust is lost when people think they can get away with cutting corners or treating others disrespectfully. It's great to be ambitious and push hard toward goals, but when individuals ignore moral boundaries, that's when they create problems for themselves and their organizations. When I was starting out in business, there was a guy I knew who was obsessively ambitious. He told me, "I'm going to be the toughest SOB ever because that's the only way to make it." He had great energy and intelligence, and he gave the impression of a worldbeater who would let nothing stop him. In fact, all he ended up doing was wasting his energy and ambition on get-rich-quick schemes that never panned out. He was very similar to corporate leaders who are always looking for angles and attempting to manipulate others.

8. Be Patient

Speed kills, especially when it comes to building trust. Don't become frustrated if you start implementing trust bank activities and everyone doesn't immediately respond with love and kisses. As I've emphasized throughout this book, creating trust isn't a quick fix. Trust emerges from a series of actions over time; it's the cumulative power of these actions that helps change stakeholders' minds about a company or strengthens their faith in and respect for a company.

Therefore, when you start putting the lessons of this book into action, don't expect too much too soon. Instead, expect a lot in the long run. If you're persistent and consistent in your trust-building efforts, it will pay off for the organization in significant ways.

9. Take Action as an Individual (Not Just as an Organization)

Though my recommendations are designed to be used by companies to restore and strengthen trust, they can also be used by individuals. It's great if you're a CEO or another organizational leader who can implement trust strategies on a large scale, but even if you're a newly minted MBA starting out on your first job, you can put this information to use.

Anyone in an organization can suggest a charitable effort that the company can sponsor or form a volunteer group for a worthy cause. People can make a conscious effort to treat direct reports with more respect or be more honest with customers. They can attempt to listen better and develop their communication skills.

Many of you may also be in a position to sell the company on trust-building activities. You may be inspired to come up with a plan that will restore trust with the media or become involved in a worthwhile cause. Whatever it is, be aware that to sell your plan to management, you need to provide it with sound business reasons for moving forward. It's possible that your management team is skeptical of do-gooder activities or is preoccupied with major business problems. If you make a presentation that focuses on the need for corporate altruism or the importance of treating people humanely, you may not make your sale. Though some leaders really grasp the concepts discussed in this book, others may not. For this reason, back up your trust arguments with business ones. As you've learned from the various examples I've provided, there are plenty of business benefits that result from trust-related activities.

10. Be Willing to Give Rather Than Receive When Appropriate

The implications of this commandment might strike business people as counterintuitive. I'm suggesting that there are certain situations when companies must spend money without ever receiving a direct return on this expenditure. Everything doesn't have to be measured by return-on-investment. There are instances when it makes sense to lose money on a "transaction." For instance, a veteran employee who contributed a great deal to the company is asked to leave because of a restructuring; the policy dictates he should receive X dollars, but the reality is that this is insufficient considering his contributions over the years. The company should voluntarily give him what he deserves, even though it is under no obligation to do so.

Northwestern Mutual is a company that has consistently followed this commandment, enjoying unusually good relationships with customers. The following story illustrates why this is so. A man tried to buy a life insurance policy for his newborn daughter, but the man's doctor failed to respond to the company's repeated requests for the baby's medical records. As a result, weeks went by without a policy being issued. Then the man called the representative, who immediately explained that the man's doctor had failed to supply them with the records. The man told her he was calling to tell them not go forward with the policy because his baby daughter had just died from Sudden Infant Death Syndrome.

This representative was upset, and after she got off the phone, she asked a claim analyst to investigate the situation to see if they could do anything for the father, and the analyst talked to her manager about the case. Together they decided that if they had received the records from the doctor (which the doctor finally sent after another request), they would have issued the policy. Therefore, Northwestern Mutual decided to issue the policy for the deceased child and paid the claim.

Prudential Financial is another company that is willing to give without asking anything in return. The Prudential "Spirit of Community Initiative" is a highly ambitious undertaking, a series of

programs designed to encourage young people to become involved in their communities. The Prudential Spirit of Community
Awards, for instance, is the largest youth recognition program
based on volunteer community service. Prudential also commissioned the Center for Creative Leadership to design a leadership
training program for high school students interested in solving
community problems—this has become The Prudential Youth
Leadership Institute. These and other related efforts require Prudential's financial support as well as a significant commitment of
time and resources. There is no direct benefit for Prudential, except that it is helping young people recognize the importance of
community and, no doubt, Prudential employees feel good about
being part of this effort.

Certainly companies can't give away the store and stay in
business. They can, however, be alert for situations where it
makes more sense to give than to receive. Some decisions can't
be made by the numbers. Companies like Prudential and Northwestern Mutual that show generosity benefit in ways that may be
difficult to measure, but are as real as money in the bank. Someone once said that integrity could be defined as *doing the right
thing when no one is looking.* From an organizational standpoint,
it's doing the right thing even when it doesn't make perfect financial sense.

A Good Trend

These ten commandments should be easier to observe now and
in the coming years than they were in the recent past. If anything
good emerged from all the financial and corporate scandals, it
has been a growing awareness of the value of trust. In former
presidential adviser David Gergen's book, *Eyewitness to Power,* he
makes the point that leaders used to assume that they had people's trust, but given all the cynicism and skepticism out there,
they now have to earn it.

In business as well as politics, leaders are more focused on saying and doing things that create trust. This "trust consciousness" is a good development, in that people often cause others to doubt them not because they're bad people but because they just weren't thinking when they took action. They may have inadvertently said something that offended a minority group or pushed through a program that hurt the environment. Thinking about trust is the first step toward creating it.

More important, it has allowed companies to take the next step from thinking to doing. It's rare these days to find a major organization that isn't involved in some type of charitable endeavor. In many companies, human resources has taken the lead in providing employees with a greater range of benefits than ever before. More organizations are not only creating value or belief statements but enacting programs and policies to ensure that these statements govern work behavior.

Perhaps most significantly, business schools seem to be focusing more on ethics than ever before. For the first time, students entering Northwestern University's Kellogg School of Management will take a ten-day course that includes emphasis on business ethics and values. Other MBA programs have started placing greater emphasis on classes about the social responsibility of business and ethical leadership behavior.

I'm not naive enough to believe that there won't be any more Enrons or that all CEOs will step up to the plate and achieve the proper balance between values and results. For every Johnson & Johnson, there's going to be a company that is myopically focused on short-term results. Still, my hope is that organizations are more *aware* of the importance of trust and are more willing than ever before to do what is necessary to *earn* it.

Golin/Harris Trust
Survey Results

Key Learnings

- **2002: Crisis of trust in business reached epidemic proportions**

  - **69%** of Americans say there is a crisis of trust in business and they don't know whom to trust anymore.

  - **38%** believe CEOs are doing the right things and all they can to restore trust in American business, compared to **62%** who do not think CEOs are doing enough.

- **2003: Trust in American business remains low...but shows signs of improvement**

  - **40%** say they trust business less than they did a year ago, compared to **10%** who say they trust business more than a year ago.

  - **37%** believe that business is heading in the right direction in rebuilding trust, compared to **17%** who think business is heading in the wrong direction on trust.

  - **46%** – nearly half of Americans – now believe CEOs are doing the right things to restore trust, up **8%** from August 2002.

  - **53%** – just over half of Americans – believe business has learned its lesson, will behave differently, and is going to be more trustworthy in the future.

Key Learnings

- **Trust has a direct <u>positive</u> impact on brand preference and loyalty**

  – **39%** of Americans say they would definitely or probably <u>start</u> doing business with a company or <u>increase</u> their business specifically because the company is trustworthy.

- **The loss of trust has an even greater direct <u>negative</u> impact on the brand**

  – **53%** say they would definitely or probably <u>stop</u> doing business with a company, <u>reduce</u> their volume of business, or <u>switch</u> to a competitor because of doubts about trustworthiness.

- **By making deposits in its "trust bank," a company has reputation assets to sustain loyalty and preference when trust is challenged**

  – **83%** agree that they are <u>more likely</u> to give a company they trust the benefit of the doubt and listen to its side of the story before making a judgment when questions are raised about corporate behavior.

Key Learnings

- **Women are slightly tougher about trust than men**
    - **43%** of women vs. **37%** of men trust business less than a year ago.
    - **33%** of women vs. **43%** of men think business is heading in the right direction on trust.

- **Younger Americans are more trusting than older Americans**
    - **48%** of people under age 35 vs. **56%** of people over age 35 would stop, decrease, or switch business from a company because of distrust.
    - **51%** under age 35 vs. **43%** over age 35 agree CEOs are doing enough to rebuild trust.

- **College-educated Americans hold business to a somewhat higher standard on trust**
    - **45%** of college-educated vs. **57%** of high school–educated Americans agree that business has learned its lessons and will be more trustworthy in the future.
    - **50%** of college-educated vs. **34%** of high school–educated Americans trust business less today than a year ago.

- **The greater the income, the greater the importance of trust**
    - **54%** of people with household incomes over $90,000 vs. **46%** between $45,000 and $90,000 vs. **34%** under $45,000 would start or increase business with a company because of trust.
    - **66%** over $90,000 vs. **61%** between $45,000 and $90,000 vs. **49%** under $45,000 would stop, decrease, or switch business because of distrust.

March 2002:
Crisis of Trust Becomes Critical

"Recent economic events have caused a crisis of confidence and trust in the way we do business in America. I just don't know whom to trust anymore. From now on I'm going to be more careful and cynical about what I believe, and I'm going to hold businesses to a higher standard in their behavior and communications."

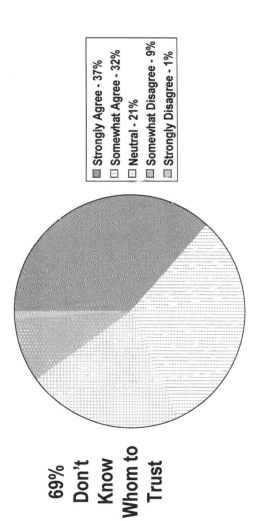

69% Don't Know Whom to Trust

- Strongly Agree - 37%
- Somewhat Agree - 32%
- Neutral - 21%
- Somewhat Disagree - 9%
- Strongly Disagree - 1%

March 2003:
Trust in Business Remains Low...

"Compared to a year ago, do you trust American business more, less, or about the same?"

40%
Trust Business Less Than a Year Ago

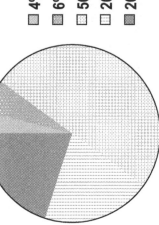

- ▣ 4% - Trust a Lot More
- ▣ 6% - Trust a Little More
- ▢ 50% - Trust About the Same
- ▢ 20% - Trust a Little Less
- ▣ 20% - Trust a Lot Less

. . .But Is Showing Signs of Improvement

"Do you think American companies are heading in the right direction or wrong direction in rebuilding trust in their businesses?"

37%
Say Business
Is Heading
in Right
Direction for
Rebuilding
Trust

- 6% - Strongly in Right Direction
- 31% - Somewhat in Right Direction
- 46% - Can't Decide Direction
- 6% - Somewhat in Wrong Direction
- 11% - Strongly in Wrong Direction

CEOs Are Regaining Trust. . .Slowly

"CEOs are doing the right things and all they can and should to restore trust in American business."

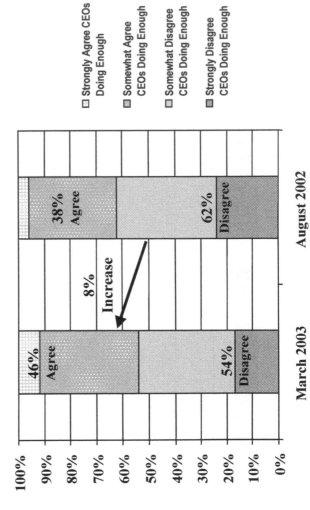

229

Trust Can Build or Bust a Brand

"How likely are you to START doing business with a company or INCREASE your business specifically because the company is trustworthy?"

"How likely are you to STOP doing business with a company, REDUCE your business, or SWITCH to a competitor specifically because you question the company's trustworthiness?"

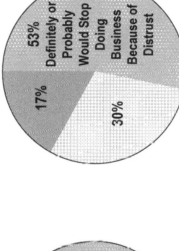

40% Definitely or Probably Would Do Business Because of Trust

22%

38%

▨ Definitely or Probably Would Do Business

☐ Possibly Would Do Business

▨ Definitely or Probably Would Not Do Business

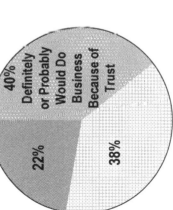

53% Definitely or Probably Would Stop Doing Business Because of Distrust

17%

30%

▨ Definitely or Probably Would Stop Doing Business

☐ Possibly Would Stop Doing Business

▨ Definitely or Probably Would Not Stop Doing Business

230

Deposits in Your Trust Bank Pay Dividends When You Need Them Most

82%
Will Give a
Company They Trust
The Benefit of the Doubt When
Behavior
Is Questioned

18%
Disagree

55%
Somewhat
Agree

27%
Strongly
Agree

"Every business has its ups and downs and experiences crises, conflicts, and questions about its behavior.

"In these cases, I'm more likely to give a company I trust the benefit of the doubt and listen to its side of the story before making a judgment."

Cautious Optimism That Business Will Become More Trustworthy

"American business really learned its lessons from the scandals over the past two years. I think business is cleaning up its act, will behave differently, and is going to be more trustworthy in the future."

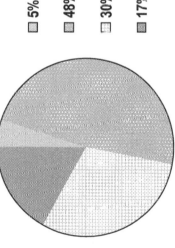

53%
Agree That
Business Has
Learned Its
Lessons and
Will Be More
Trustworthy
in the Future

☐ 5% - Strongly Agree

▨ 48% - Somewhat Agree

☐ 30% - Somewhat Disagree

▨ 17% - Strongly Disagree

Women Are a Little Tougher on Trust

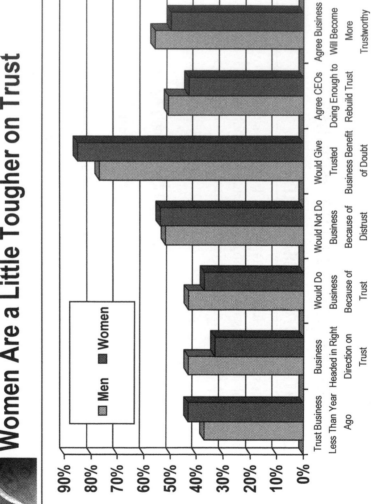

Younger People Are More Trusting

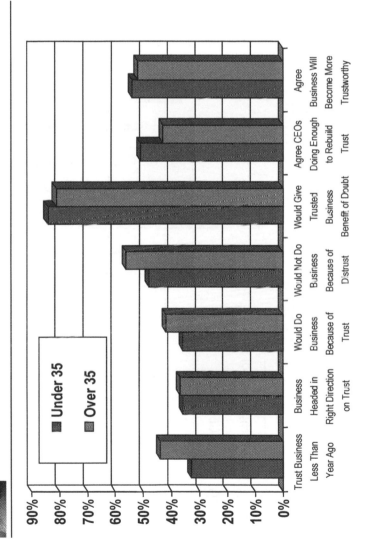

Higher Education, Lower Trust

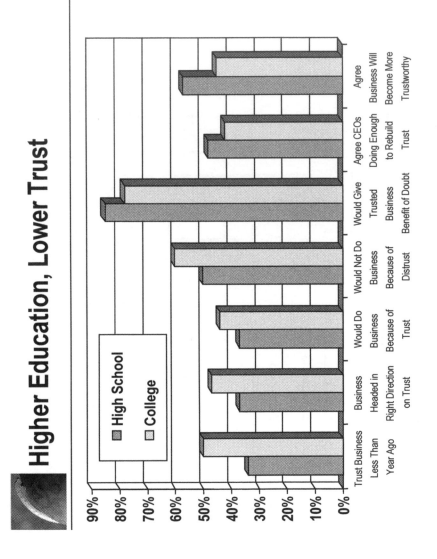

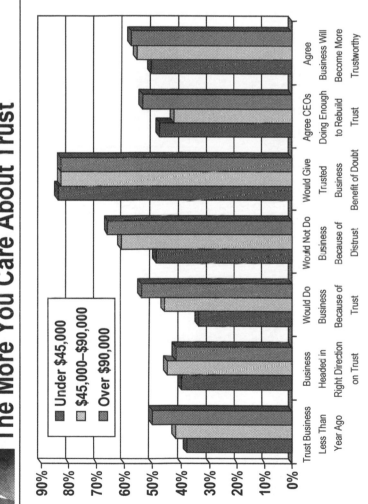

The More Money You Make, The More You Care About Trust

Legend:
- Under $45,000
- $45,000–$90,000
- Over $90,000

Categories:
- Trust Business Less Than Year Ago
- Business Headed in Right Direction on Trust
- Would Do Business Because of Trust
- Would Not Do Business Because of Distrust
- Would Give Trusted Business Benefit of Doubt
- Agree CEOs Doing Enough to Rebuild Trust
- Agree Business Will Become More Trustworthy

Who Is Most Demanding on Trust? Women, Over 35, College, Upper Income

Perception	All	Men	Women	Under 35	Over 35	High School	College	Under $45K	$45 - $90K	Over $90K
Trust business less than a year ago	40%	37%	43%	33%	44%	34%	50%	38%	42%	50%
Business headed in right direction on trust	37%	43%	33%	36%	37%	37%	47%	40%	45%	42%
Would start/ increase business because of trust	39%	43%	37%	36%	42%	37%	44%	34%	46%	54%
Would stop, decrease, or switch business because of distrust	53%	52%	54%	48%	56%	50%	60%	49%	61%	66%
Would give trusted business benefit of the doubt	82%	77%	85%	84%	81%	85%	78%	84%	83%	83%
Agree CEOs are doing enough to rebuild trust	46%	51%	43%	51%	43%	48%	42%	48%	43%	54%
Agree business will become more trustworthy in the future	53%	56%	50%	54%	52%	57%	45%	51%	56%	58%

Bottom Line

- The trajectory of trust is "getting better," but American business still has a long way to go before the trust situation is "good."

- Americans are "cautiously optimistic" that business is setting its house in order, but <u>execution is the key</u>. The public has little tolerance for "promises made" . . . only "promises kept."

- Trust is shifting from "brand infrastructure" – part of the "streets and sidewalks" of the brand that must be kept in good repair – to trust as a "brand asset" that is fundamental to fostering loyalty and preference.

- 2003 will see a shift away from reactive "trust busting" crisis management to proactive "trust building" to enhance reputation, confidence, differentiation, and value.

- As companies become more sophisticated in their trust management, they will begin to develop audience-specific trust-building strategies designed to address the varied concerns and desires of different demographic groups.

About the Survey

This survey was developed by Golin/Harris International and fielded with InsightExpress. It was conducted in 2002 and again in 2003 with an online survey methodology and has a plus-or-minus 5 percent margin of error. The survey was conducted of a cross-section of the U.S. population with 300 consumers over the age of 18.

B

Golin/Harris Trust Index

Golin/Harris Trust Index

Integration of "Whom do you trust the most? Whom do you trust the least? Is your trust in each increasing? Is your trust in each decreasing?"

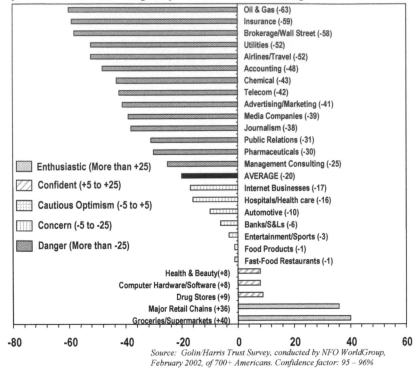

Oil & Gas (-63)
Insurance (-59)
Brokerage/Wall Street (-58)
Utilities (-52)
Airlines/Travel (-52)
Accounting (-48)
Chemical (-43)
Telecom (-42)
Advertising/Marketing (-41)
Media Companies (-39)
Journalism (-38)
Public Relations (-31)
Pharmaceuticals (-30)
Management Consulting (-25)
AVERAGE (-20)
Internet Businesses (-17)
Hospitals/Health care (-16)
Automotive (-10)
Banks/S&Ls (-6)
Entertainment/Sports (-3)
Food Products (-1)
Fast-Food Restaurants (-1)
Health & Beauty(+8)
Computer Hardware/Software (+8)
Drug Stores (+9)
Major Retail Chains (+36)
Groceries/Supermarkets (+40)

Enthusiastic (More than +25)
Confident (+5 to +25)
Cautious Optimism (-5 to +5)
Concern (-5 to -25)
Danger (More than -25)

-80   -60   -40   -20   0   20   40   60

Source: Golin/Harris Trust Survey, conducted by NFO WorldGroup, February 2002, of 700+ Americans. Confidence factor: 95 – 96%

Pinpointing a Business Sector's Trust Profile – This chart is a unique and powerful indicator of an industry's trust profile in today's economy. The Golin/Harris Trust Index score is derived by combining each business sector's degree and direction of trust as measured by the four trust variables – trust most, trust least, trust increasing, and trust decreasing. Using this scale, Golin/Harris helps individual companies to understand the challenges, opportunities, and urgencies of its own strength as a trusted brand, instituting strategies and tactics to increase trust across all stakeholders – customers, partners, employees, investors, and the communities in which they do business.

For more information, contact: Mark Rozeen, Golin/Harris, 212-309-0658, mrozeen@golinharris.com

Index

241

Lightning Source UK Ltd.
Milton Keynes UK
UKHW032149090919
349456UK00003B/1238/P